Point Place
just a couple of years ago

contents

HOODLUMS, THIEVES, CROOKS
and other
POINT PLACE RESIDENTS

The Point Place State Bank

Toledoans were coming to the Point in droves. Not only were they spending their days along the wind swept shores of the Ottawa and Maumee Rivers, they were investing in property and cottages in Point Place. With plans already in the works for expansion, Willow Beach Toledo's newest amusement park was prospering beyond the owners expectations. Amid this huge influx of people and money into the Point, several of the Point's leading residents decided to ride the wave of expansion, and open a bank.

Pledging $30,000 of their own money, Kleis, Stader, Weiss, Cummerow, Eikost, and seven other prominent Point Placer's signed the bank's Papers of Incorporation. The proposed bank's financial plans were presented to the Ohio state bank examiner, and once they were approved the bank was one step closer to opening. Some residents of the Point regarded this announcement as just one more in a long string of April Fool's jokes, but other inhabitants applauded the financial sense of the petitioners. The Point's young and old responded with their savings when the bank finally opened its doors.

Point Place State Bank was located at 4901 Summit Street at the corner of 116th Street. From the author's collection.

Several scoundrels from the greater Toledo area also applauded the opening of the bank in Point Place, but for a different reason …. They were going to rob the bank.

Parking their stolen Dodge sedan in front of the bank and with guns drawn they entered the bank and shouted *"…put your hands in the air, this is a stick-up…"* The only customer in the bank at the time was 10 year old Dorothy Kolling, who was making a savings deposit for her sister, Thelma. Trembling at the sound of the gruff voices behind her and realizing the implications, Dorothy quickly stuffed her sister's money into her blouse, raised her hands and faced the robbers. Later, Dorothy told her mother that she was more afraid of loosing her sister's money than the robbers. *"Thelma would have killed me."*

Dorothy [Kolling] Schuster. Courtesy of her daughter Deborah Pryba.

In the excitement of the moment, with their guns leveled at Dorothy and Frank Kahle the cashier, the robbers remembered that they had forgotten to wear masks and quickly raised their free hand to cover their faces. With Dorothy standing right in front of the cashier's cage the bank robber was unable to force his way through the teller's cage and had to awkwardly scale the wall that partitioned the bank. As the robber scuffed his way over the wall, Kahle later remembers thinking *"..I could have shot him any time, but I didn't have a gun."*

Once he climbed the wall the robber wasn't much better at intimidating the cashier. With the gun shaking in his hand and the other hand trying to hide his features the robber handed a huge white canvas bag to Kahle and told him to fill it up. Seeing all that money, the robber withdrew his hand from his face, and started removing hand-fulls of bills from the cash drawer, and stuffing them in the white canvas bag. Spotting another drawer that was filled with $1,500 in small change; the bag eventually became so heavy that Kahle couldn't hold it up anymore. Kahle dropped the bag to the polished wooden floorboards scattering the money all over the floor.

Obviously the bank robbery was not going as planned. The robber ordered Kahle to scoop the money up, and then to add insult to injury Kahle had to help carry the money to the waiting car. Dorothy, with her hands still in the air, and Kahle dragging the canvas bag filled with money out the bank's entrance, the robbers and their white canvas bag finally made their escape.

Watching the last act of this comedy was Mrs. F. L. Jewett of 104th Street. In true Nancy Drew fashion, the 23 year old threw her sport roadster into the pursuit, while carloads of police alerted to the robbery, were speeding through the quiet neighborhoods of the Point looking for the Dodge sedan and the robbers. Running through traffic lights and skidding around corners the robbers pushed the old Dodge to its limit as they turned onto Suder. Realizing that they couldn't outrun the roadster, they quickly brought the Dodge to a stop and threatened Mrs. Jewett with their guns. After turning left on Manhattan Boulevard the robbers were recognized by a group of men repairing the street. A little further on the bandits stopped, raised their guns, and shouted to Mrs. Jewett *"We'll kill you if you don't go back."* Continuing the chase from what she considered a safer distance, she watched the men abandon the Dodge, and plunge into Detwiler Marsh off Manhattan.

Evidently the white canvas bag was just too heavy to carry, because when Mrs. Jewett returned with the police to the place where the robbers entered the marsh, the police quickly found several twenty dollar bills in the tall grass. Following the trail of spilled money the white canvas bag was recovered a short distance off Manhattan, covered with mud and containing $2,071. When asked by the police, why after being threatened, she didn't stop, she simply replied *"...why, that was our money, my husbands and mine, and if I would have lost that money my husband would have killed me."*

the Peach Orchard

In 1891 Nathan Moore and Son's Cherry Street nursery was less than a half mile's walk along the old Indian trail to Detroit. It was almost all downhill to the Ottawa River, and on hot summer days it was a refreshing way to spend your lunch hour .

It had been an extremely hot spring when John Weitzel went to work for Nathan Moore in his nursery. John was used to the long hours required to meet the customer's needs and the hard physical labor that was necessary. When the nursery crew planted shrubs and trees at customer's houses over on the *"wood"* streets, even the *"swells"* would offer them a beer or two at the end of the day. But not Nathan Moore.

After a long day, several of the boys in John's nursery crew would stop at Isaac Matzinger's saloon at Stickney Avenue and the Ottawa River and have several schooners of draft beer. They were still there long after sunset when John and his new best buddy, Jacob Kaiser, would, instead of going home, row back up the Ottawa and visit Moore's nursery.

After several more beers than they could pay for, the darkness that enveloped Cherry Street was the perfect cover for what they had planned. Every step they took up Detroit to Cherry Street was memorable as the alcohol began to pound the same walking rhythm in their heads. By the time they got to the nursery they had forgotten just what their plan was.

Making the theft up as they entered the nursery they quickly gathered seventy peach trees, one evergreen, and a small cart to help them get their loot back to their row boat. The newspaper doesn't mention what the trip was like as they rowed back down the Ottawa River to Matzinger's Saloon, but one can only imagine. As they tied the row boat to a small sapling that was growing on the bank they quickly sold twenty of their new found peach trees to a man named Hanzler for two dollars.

The next morning, lying next to their rowboat, half in the mud and half in the water, Weitzel and Kaiser had only the faintest recollection of the night before. They didn't exactly know what had happened, but they were suffering the consequences. It wasn't till they sat up and their eyes began to focus that they saw the peach trees and the single evergreen still in their rowboat. Looking at each other with bewilderment written all over their faces, it finally dawned on them that they had stolen the trees and spent the entire proceeds, the whole two dollars on beer.

Several people had witnessed their carefully planned theft, and an arrest warrant was issued for John Weitzel and Jacob Kaiser. Arrested, and then released on their word, it wasn't till August that they appeared before the police court with clerk W. H. Cook presiding.

John Weitzel pleaded guilty and acknowledged his part in the theft, but Jacob Kaiser denied that the event ever took place. Mr. Stein who was a book-keeper for the Toledo brewery Grasser & Brand acted as attorney of record for Mr. Kaiser. It wasn't long into Jacob Kaiser's cross-examination that he finally admitted helping Mr. Weitzel carry the trees from the nursery to the rowboat. However, the rest of the evening's events were still missing from his memory.

Cook quickly fined Jacob Kaiser five dollars and court costs. And when he came to John Weitzel he saved the best till last …. Twenty dollars court costs and twenty days in the county workhouse. Justice in Toledo. 1891.

∗LENK WINE CO.,∗

TOLEDO, OHIO.

GROWERS OF AND DEALERS IN ALL KINDS OF

AMERICAN ◉ WINES,

LAKE ERIE ISLANDS WINES A SPECIALTY.

DRY ∗ AND ∗ SWEET ∗ CATAWBAS,

Delaware, Norton's Virginia Seedling, Ives' Seedling, Claret and Port.

Lenk Wine Company was located at Tremainsville near the intersection of Detroit Avenue and the Ottawa River. From the author's collection.

Dr. Joseph P. Moran and the Toledo Harbor Light

Born in Springvalley, Illinois in 1895, Moran served in France after enlisting in the war to end all wars. He was educated at Boston's Tuft's Medical School where he graduated with honors, and in 1934 he was brutally murdered in Toledo, Ohio. Dr. Joseph P. Moran had an exceptionally short life for someone who was in so much trouble with both sides of the law.

Soon after opening his medical practice in Lasalle, Illinois, Dr. Moran was convicted of performing illegal operations and spent three of his thirty-nine years in Joliet State Prison. While he was in prison he continued his medical practice and perfected many of the skills that would endear him to the Chicago underworld.

After leaving the Illinois state prison, Moran journeyed north and set-up his medical practice in Chicago where he would be close to many of his clients that he met while incarcerated. Word soon spread throughout the mid-west that Dr. Moran was the man to see if you wanted your fingerprints to disappear and your appearance changed. His practice was not limited to just plastic surgery and for a fee of just over five thousand dollars he operated and saved the life of badly wounded John Hamilton. Shot-up in a botched East Chicago bank robbery, Dillinger dumped the bleeding Hamilton on his doorstep and said to Moran *"… you better save his life …"* Afterwards Hamilton was so appreciative of having his life returned to him that he reentered the world of bank robbing. After Hamilton was wounded in the *"Little Bohemia"* confrontation in Wisconsin, Dillinger brought his fatally wounded partner to a backroom of a Chicago saloon and summoned Moran. Dr. Moran took one look at Hamilton and walked out to the bar. According to the word circulating through Chicago, Moran told Dillinger *"… that Hamilton was already a dead man, why waste your money."*

In the Spring of 1933 the Barker gang kidnapped a wealthy Minneapolis brewer, William Hamm Jr., for a $100,000 ransom. The money was paid and the Barker Gang was celebrating when they found out that Doc Barker had left a single fingerprint at the crime scene and that Hoover and the FBI had traced the print directly to Doc Barker. Pictures of Doc and Freddie Barker, Alvin Karpis, and other known gang members were soon appearing in all of the popular magazines as well as the post office.

An example of the notoriety that followed the gang was noticed in Toledo and ruined the career of one of Lucas County's sheriffs. Harry Campbell, one of Alvin Karpis's criminal companions was arrested in Toledo in 1936. Fearing a leak in his plans, Hoover and four car loads of his G-Men flew into Toledo, alerted the newspapers, and raided Campbell's apartment on Monroe Street. The tip to Campbell's location came from Karpis whom Hoover had already jailed, and Karpis was traced by his frequent purchases of bichloride of mercury to treat a virulent form of syphilis. Campbell had been living in the Monroe Street apartment under the name Bob Miller.

Courtesy of the F. B. I.

" *I can take it,*" said Sheriff James O'Reilly after Toledo's newspapers printed revelations that Sheriff O'Reilly and Campbell had been on friendly terms for the last five months. As the story unfolded Mr. Jaworski, a reporter for the News Bee, said *"I had gone out to check the details of the Campbell arrest. I walked through the Goulet Grill and ran into Sheriff O'Reilly in the back yard. He[O'Reilly] was coming down from the apartment adjoining the apartment Campbell had occupied.* It was then that Sheriff O'Reilly said *"I've been drinking beer with him plenty of times but I never knew who he was. I had never seen a picture of the man."* Checking O'Reilly's story one reporter found a deputy sheriff who said that the circular had been on O'Reilly's bulletin board but was removed after Hoover arrested Campbell.

It was during the capture of Campbell that J. Edgar Hoover told reporters that *"Campbell was well known in Toledo underworld circles. He made this city [Toledo] one of his principal hangouts and it was to Toledo that the Barker-Karpis gang came after the kidnapping of the St. Paul brewer."* It was also during the aftermath of the Campbell raid that Hoover said he had been told that Dr. Moran was *".. buried at the bottom of Lake Erie."* Later the BLADE said *"… The first time the gang came to Toledo they stayed at Point Place and at a downtown hotel. It was in Toledo that the fingerprint operations took place."*

A Point Place tavern that could have been one of Dr. Moran's hangouts on 131st Street. From the author's collection.

According to sources close to the gang members, after they had their picture plastered all over, they decided to call Dr. Moran for a few changes in their appearance and fingerprints. Working in a cottage on 131st Street in Point Place, Dr. Moran sedated Barker and Karpis with large injections of morphine to lessen the pain and went to work. Dr. Moran performed surgery on their noses, chins, and jaw line. Finishing the surgery he started on their fingerprints. Karpis would later say that *"he froze my fingertips with cocaine and scrapped them with a scalpel. He was sharpening the ends of my finger just like you would sharpen a pencil."*

By this time in his career Dr. Moran was drinking to excess and was probably drunk during the entire operations. The facial surgery left scars that wouldn't heal correctly and both of the men were in severe pain from their fingers that were continuously infected. Fred Barkis was overheard saying *"I'm going to kill Moran as soon as I can hold a gun."*

It was in late August of 1934 that Dr. Moran, while enjoying the company of several ladies of the evening, bragged *"I've got this whole gang in the hollow of my hand, right here."* The ladies called Barker and Karpis and when they arrived they took Moran for a ride …. a boat ride. Barker's quote was *"Doc and I shot the son-of-a-bitch."*

An article from a 1936 issue of the Toledo NewsBee by Robert S. Brown strongly suggested that Dr. Joseph Moran could be found somewhere off Toledo Harbor Light. From the author's collection.

the featherweight championship fight
with
Toledoan Fred Green and the guy from Detroit, Harry Cobb
&
the stranger from Australia

The year was 1891 and the idle conversation throughout the bars and saloons of Toledo and Detroit was not about Thomas Edison's kinetoscope, but rather could Fred Green beat Harry Cobb. Many pugilistic battles were won and lost as the conversation ebbed and flowed around the mugs of beer and swirled amidst the thick grey cigar smoke that permeated the men and their waxed moustaches. For Toledoans the verbal outcome of any imagined contest was always the lineman for Western Union, Freddy Green. Conversely, their counterparts in Detroit always sided with Harry Cobb.

Green and Cobb, the favorites of their respective cities, were extremely dangerous men, and given the right circumstances either one could knock the other out. The ringside experts agreed without an exception, the only way to settle this once and for all was to have the two men shake hands and fight it out. The only problem was that exhibitions of pugilistic skill, or the fights, were illegal and looked down upon by polite society. However, some patrons of that same polite society were found cheering their favorite fighter from ringside.

With the bar stool experts almost coming to blows as where to stage this exhibition, both sides had ruled out Toledo's Walbridge Park. The wisest of the promoters began to slowly arrive at the conclusion that a location near the Ohio Michigan state line would ensure a double measure of safety. They reasoned that if the authorities came from Michigan they could leisurely cross into Ohio, and vice versa, thus escaping the severe legal penalties afforded by both states.

Several locations were offered, but the one that garnered the most support was the old roadhouse at the junction of Michigan Avenue and the Ottawa River. On the north side of the roadhouse was a grove of tall oaks and graceful willows that had been the setting of many German picnics and festivals. There was a slight hesitation on the Detroiter's part until someone remembered that the proprietor of the roadhouse was a sportsman and might just donate his grove and a few pints of beer.

The location was settled, and one hundred and fifty $1 tickets sold as fast as the bartender could collect the dollar bills. One of the purchasers was Ollie Pecord an excellent boxer from Toledo. Many years later, Ollie Pecord would referee one of the world's greatest heavyweight boxing contests – the Willard Dempsey fight in 1919.

Pecord and a group of Green supporters arrived early to inspect the picnic grove turned fight arena. Selecting four rather large oaks which formed a square deep within the grove, the proprietor of the roadhouse had prepared the 21 foot boxing ring by tightly stretching a stout manila line several times around each of the oaks.

A mighty cheer went up from the assembled spectators when Harry Cobb and his group of supporters arrived from Detroit. Both men stripped off their shirts, cinched their trouser belts, and prepared for battle. There was just one small problem. In their haste to arrange the fight they had forgotten to include a referee.

**Jim Hall or James Montague Furlong, Australian Heavyweight Champion.
Courtesy of Cyberboxing. Com.**

When the self appointed fight announcer asked for a volunteer *"... a towering giant of a man stepped forward. He had a barrel of a chest, tree trunks for arms, fists the size of hams, and a cauliflower ear. He said his name was Jim Hall."* A slight murmur of recognition streaked through the crowd. This was the famous Montague James Furlong, the Australian Heavyweight Champion that had knocked out Bob Fitzsimmons in Sydney. Bowing to his fans, Hall received congratulations from the crowd as he made his way to the ring. No one would expect that this great fighter, who just happened to be in Toledo, to referee gratis. Almost by magic a hat was quickly circulated through the crowd and fifty dollars was collected.

The fighters were introduced in the ring by the referee; shook hands, and before Hall could drop his hand signifying the start of the fight two gentlemen from Erie, Michigan, both deputy sheriffs, arrived ringside. Sooner than they could arrest the startled spectators and participants, the entire crowd moved as one, manila rope and all to the Ohio side of the grove. In less than thirty minutes the fight was about to begin again, and the last word from the deputies as they disappeared down the dusty mud road was that they were going for the law ... the Ohio law.

Hall dropped his fist and the two fighters who had been facing each other were now circling each other and as the opportunity presented itself landing blow upon blow. Round after round passed as the anxious lookouts paced back and forth outside the grove watching the horizon for a cloud of dust forming on the Toledo road.

Fought under the auspices of the Marquis of Queensbury Rules, the boys punched and counterpunched each other, round after round. After twenty rounds in the hot afternoon sun of an August summer Hall said the fight was over. He called both fighters to the center of the ring, raised both of their bloodied fists, and announced the fight was a draw. The spectators were on their feet stomping and cheering for one of the best fights they had ever seen. The cheering went on for what seemed like hours till Hall raised his hand for silence. When the crowd quieted he said *"Boys, you better get going, I think I hear someone coming."* The manila rope was gathered in, and the grove which was teaming with life just moments before, was deserted.

Within minutes, there wasn't a table to be had at Jones' Roadhouse, and in the bar room it was standing room only as glass after glass was raised to Green and Cobb.

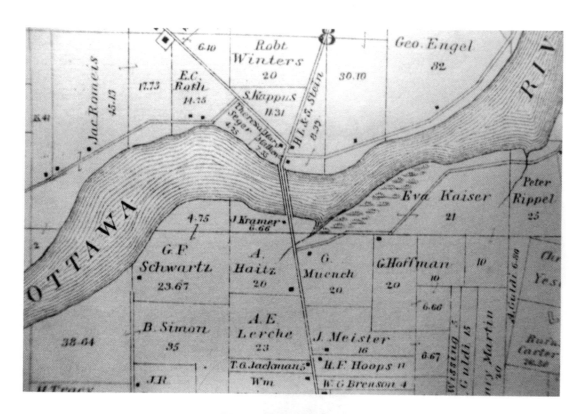

Picnic Grove Location

The map shows the location of the picnic grove and roadhouse where the fight took place. N. Michigan Avenue intersects Summit Street just before Bay View Park. After crossing Manhattan Boulevard N. Michigan Avenue becomes the Ten Mile Creek Road. Today, both roads are called Suder Avenue. The early written reports of this contest all mention a roadhouse [saloon] and the Toledo city directory for 1900 lists David Jones's Saloon at the intersection of N. Michigan Avenue [Suder Avenue] and Ten Mile Creek [Ottawa River]. The surrounding property owners were all first generation German, and this area would have been the logical choice for the German musical festivals.

From the Point Place Memories by Marcia King. *Remember the prize fights held in the back of this place [Thompson's Inn]? When the sheriff tried to stop them, they would move the arena over the state line into Michigan. Clarence and Stella Eikost.*

Characters, Stories, and other lies.

Cam King's boathouse or fishing shanty at the end of 145th Street and 326th Street. Cam had boats for rent, bait, anything that you would need for a day on the lake. Everything was destroyed in the Flood of 1972. Courtesy of the Point Place Heritage Society.

Edgewater Gun Club

Tournament with a Little Home Talent, July 23, 1903. Courtesy of Ralph Kern and the Point Place Heritage Society.

The pigeon shoots were held at Billy Gertz's Restaurant way out in Point Place at the end of the dirt road. Shooters would come from all over, some from as far away as Napoleon, Ohio to compete. According to several newspaper accounts the gentlemen would pay an entry fee, and an official would record the number of "kills." The winner would be announced, and sometimes money prizes were given to the fifth or sixth place.

Toledo *BEE*, June 25, 1899
"… Last Sunday Gus Webber and W. C. Gertz had a contest at clay pigeons. Webber won in each of the two matches of 24 birds, double rise. … Gertz then best Webber in a

25 bird contest. … The lady astonished some of the masculine shooters by the way in which she handled the gun, without practice."

The Edgewater Gun Club circa 1910. On the left the gentleman with the white shirt, dark vest and tie is Horace "Boss" Kern, and sitting on the grass on the right is Lemuel "Roy" Kern. Courtesy of Ralph Kern and the Point Place Heritage Society.

The dead birds were gathered up by the neighborhood kids, placed in piles, that were sometimes three or four feet in diameter and at least as high. Later, as the day unfolded the boys would clean the birds and roast them for the gang of marksmen that would remain well into the evening at Billy Gertz's. As they left for the street car to take them back to Toledo they all carried flour sacks full of birds.

Records were kept of these events and several ledger books have been given to the Point Place Heritage Society by Point Place resident Richard Pheatt. The ledgers were kept by brothers Gideon Kelsey and Zeulon Converse Pheatt for the years 1860, 1861, and 1863.

Hunting in Point Place 1921. From l – r: Ed Bently, Frank Buroway, Mr. sting, Fred Condon, Ed Stumpmeyer, Mr. Williamson. Courtesy of Ron Richardson and the Point Place Heritage Society.

Rabbit hunting in Point Place 1921. From l – r: Mr. Williamson, William Condon, Mr. Sting, Ed Bently, Ed Stumpmeyer, and Frank Buroway. Courtesy of Ron Richardson and the Point Place Heritage Society.

1921
Port of Toledo
Development

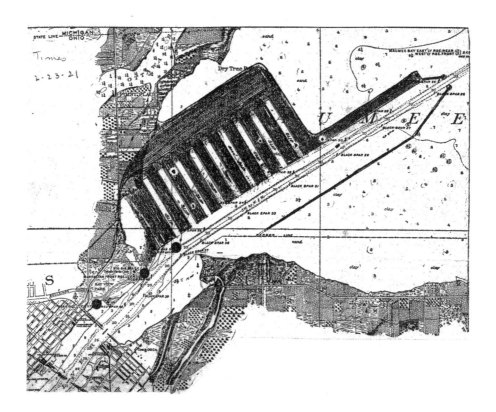

Colonel William P. Judson the division engineer for the Army planned for future port expansion by moving the shipping terminals to Point Place. According to the Toledo *TIMES* article, Colonel Judson was in charge of all the early work necessary to straighten the Maumee River channel, and *"was thoroughly acquainted with the problems involved in the plan."*

Each slip would be 4,000 feet in length and there would be 39 miles of railyard at the western end of the piers. Grain elevators, coal dock with loading and unloading equipment, repair shops along with a dry dock are included in the proposal. With no bridges to hinder the flow of traffic in and out of the port the railroads would have exceptional access. Everything has been planned for said Col. Judson, *"and the plan would compromise riparian rights with only a few landowners on the bayshore."*

Along the Water Front
George "Jake" Erd

Along The Waterfront
By George "Jake" Erd

● The Ottawa River Yacht Clubs "Farmers annual Corn Roast and Picnic" will be again held on Guard Island Sunday, September 2, 1951 with games, contests and prizes. Everyone is invited to attend. It is hinted that this will be the biggest event of them all. Come on over and find out for your self. Boats to haul passengers will leave the club dock as often as possible and there will be no charge for this service. Remember the date and please bring the picnic basket, swimming suit and change of diapers for the baby. We'll be looking for you.

Next in line for the island is the Put-In-Bay annual grape festival, Saturday and Sunday, September 8 & 9. The outstanding event of the season with bands and strut dances. Free entertainment and free prizes galore and a new 1951 Buick Reviera will be given away. Passenger ferries will leave from Catawaba, Port Clinton, Sandusky and Lakeside. Plan to attend this great event and learn the history of the islands, grapes and wine.

● Point Placers are the **Leinhardts** again as they have purchased the late Charley Singeltons homestead on the corner of 140th and Edgewater Drive and incidentally **Chuck and Dorothy** have taken over the kitchen at the O. R.Y.C., assisted by their daughter **Pat.** We sure are glad you're back folks.

● **Floyd McAtee and Ed Kennedy** have much in common, they both like swimming and boat riding, but when it comes to losing things Kennedy tops the list. He lost his shoes, shirt and cap & two weeks later I found them in my boat, tucked deep in a corner. I just misslaid them said Eddie—where I couldn't find 'em.

● **Chester "Little Jake" Sabin** is now proprietor and boss of Chet and Dale's Marine Service at 5825 Edgewater Dr. **Dale** has decided to quit the boat business and become a farmer and learn about the birds and bees and flowers the hard way.

Courtesy of TIDBITS 1951

Along The Waterfront
By George "Jake" Erd

● Over at Put-In-Bay the I.L.Y.A. Regatta was a great success, it is estimated that there were over 25,000 visitors on the island to attend this great event. Ferry boats were packed with people and cars from early morn to late at night, hauling from island to mainland, long lines of cars waited for hours to be ferried across to the island. Hundreds of boats from big new luxury yachts down to half sunken hulks lay at anchor in the harbor or tied to the many docks along the water front. We met lots of old and new friends some of whom are: **Commodore Frank Martin** of the Edison Boat Club; **Charles C. Dooree,** Buffalo; **Nick Kotts, Mike Wendel and Tony Earhardt** from Cleveland; **Russ Caulkin** and his party from Monroe; **Skipper H. L. Cooper,** Chicago; **Mr. and Mrs. Earl Stranton,** Daytona Beach, Fla. Among our many Toledo friends were: **Mr. & Mrs. Frank Rate, Mr. & Mrs. Wm. McNutt, Mr. & Mrs. Marion Meeker, Jimmy Fallon, Bud Miller, Floyd Ransom, Mr. & Mrs. Ed Madroy, Mr. & Mrs. Chet Sabin, Mr. & Mrs. Don Fisher, Mr. and Mrs. Beedee, Mr. & Mrs. Al Williams, Mr. & Mrs. Cecil Neese & Daughter Nonie, Mr. & Mrs. Ray Gibbs, Doc "Peanuts" Worley** and many other friends that were met after this article was written up and sent in. One of the funniest things I saw at the regatta was the sign on Grunkie's Park Hotel, it read: "Under (No) Management" and it the bottom of the sign it said "Rooms for Rent, specially with beds". I asked what that meant. Grunkie replied "Who wants to sleep in the bath tub. . . they can get wet enough on their boats. Fair enough".

● The grand prize of a 16 ft. Lyman outboard and motor that the O.R.Y.C. gave away at their A.Y. C. Regatta July 22, was won by **Mr. Don Duda,** 2932 Higgons St., Toledo.

● **Frank "Pontiac" Elliot** says he is being gyped this summer, with too much work to do, he has a nice new skippers hat, boat and motor and can't use them. There just ain't any rest for the wicked, I guess.

Courtesy of TIDBITS 1951

… WHAT EVER HAPPENED TO …

the Catalina Club

Purchased from the estate of Laura Thompson for $30,000 the newly chartered Catalina Club took control of Thompson's Inn, the Inn's liquor license and seven acres of surrounding land in January of 1953. The Point Place landmark was once the summer home of the Loyal Order of Moose, but the roadhouse gained notoriety during prohibition because of its waterfront location and proximity to the Michigan state line.

Ad from the Point Place Herald 1926. From the author's collection.

The Thompson's Inn as My Brother's Place. Courtesy of the Toledo Lucas County Public Library.

Alyce M. Swary of the Central Boat & Trailer Company on Upton Avenue will be President of the Catalina Club with Ed Arenson of Toledo Iron & Steel as Vice-president, and Ed Neumann from the Neumann Brother's Jewelers as treasurer. Initial plans call for over $200,000 to be invested.

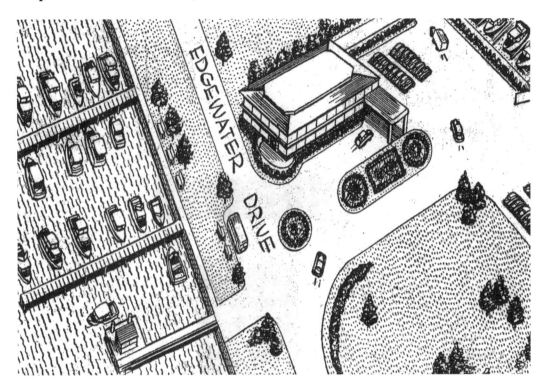

Artist's conception from the Toledo BLADE of the proposed Catalina Club.
Courtesy of John Robinson Block and the Toledo BLADE.

The proposed plans called for a complete renovation of the Thompson's Inn into an ultramodern clubhouse with facilities for a dining room, full service bar, observation lounges, clubrooms, and parking for 300 patrons. The plans called for the Inn's 7 acres to be completely landscaped to enhance the natural beauty of the waterfront, and eighty docking slips for the members and visitors boats. Winter boat storage has also been planned for in the rear of the property.

In February of 1953 the architectural firm of Britsch & Munger were retained as consultants for the Catalina Club, and according to Mrs. Alyce Swary remodeling contracts will be awarded in the near future. Forty charter members of the Catalina Club were in place as the ice left the Ottawa River in 1953.

In Jake Erd's column "Along the Waterfront" [February 5, 1953 TIDBITS] the Catalina Club was mentioned.

"I have been informed that the new $200,000 Ultra Modern Catalina Club will be a private Yacht Club. Their property is the former Thompson's Inn, settling between Webber's and Ellis's property along Edgewater Drive. The property runs from the channel of the Ottawa River to the Street and from the Street back to the Toledo Fish Company property on the Maumee Bay. The club, I'm told, will also have beautiful green lawns, flower gardens with hundreds of different kinds of flowers, shrubs, bushes, trees and so on. There is one sticker in my mind on how the officers of the club are going to build two mooring docks and one fuel service dock on 200 feet of water front property that the club has been stated to own with Jockett's dock as close as it is on one side and the end of Webber's property on the other. It may be possible, but I don't see how. Anyway, good luck to them and glad to see them on the Water Front."

A little over a year later the Catalina Club is mentioned again in Jake Erd's column "Along the Waterfront" [March 4, 1954 TIDBITS].

"The $200,000 modern Catalina Club that was supposed to be made from the former Thompson's Inn, it's a big wonderful dream that has faded away. I'm told that although the place is called the Catalina Club, it is to remain a night club open to the public from 6 pm till 2:30 am. I was also told that the reason the club could not materialize was because the water front was not large enough for one thing for the amount of boats that the club figured could be moored on their property. It's also said that the club could not dig a channel in the rear of their property to pull boats out for winter storage because they would have to cross other people's property with the digging. Our old friends, Lee and Minnie Paupard, are managers of the club until such a time the owners decide whether they are going to sell the property, keep it as a business place, or go ahead with their plans for a private club."

But by February of 1955, with the clubhouse remodeled, the docking facilities had not been completed. Lee Paupard vice-president and residential manager, who lives on the Catalina Club's property, along with Ed Neumann, president, said that the club is opening a drive for members to enhance its reputation as a public dining and dancing facility. Continuing, Mr. Neumann said that members will have their own dining and docking privileges separate from the public.

Consumer's Power Channel & Johnson's Cut

In Jake Erd's column "Along the Waterfront" [October 25, 1951 issue of TIDBITS] mention was made of Woodtick Peninsula.

"I am told that lake freighters up to 300 feet in length and of 90 coal car capacity will haul coal up to the new plant, through the new channel being dredged from the main channel to the Company's Inner – North Bay, near Erie Road. I'm told that Johnson's cut off will be closed to all traffic this fall. Johnson's cut is between Inner North Bay and Outer North Bay, near Woodtick. Let's all hope this is one mistake for small boatmen that will be corrected and the cut will be left open."

the Sulphur Spring

Since I'm in the neighborhood, have you ever seen the beautiful blue water pouring forth from the sulfur spring in the middle of the brownish water of the Maumee? The color is absolutely breathtaking, or was that the sulfur odor that took your breath away?

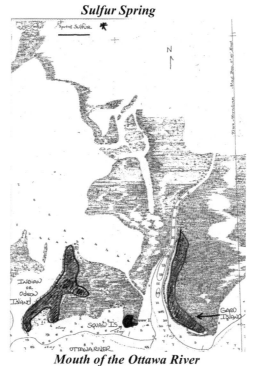

Sulfur Spring

Mouth of the Ottawa River

Sulphur Spring, Indian Is., Squaw Is., and Gard Is. at the mouth of the Ottawa River 1877. From the author's collection.

… Riffle Rock …

Guarded by a 32 pound cannon from the *GEORGE REX*, a British raider, residents of Toledo's newest waterfront development will certainly feel secure in their homes. Riffle Rock, located on a 12 acre tract of land in the Ottawa River, Toledo's newest waterfront development will be accessible from a causeway joining the island to Point Place.

Spokesperson Robert Koproski, representing Paul M. Evans, Incorporated, said that the new development has room for 27 American style homes built in the style of the English Boston Bay residences. Weeping willow trees will be planted along the shoreline to enhance the feeling of relaxation along with concrete curbs and roadways. Sanitary and storm sewers coupled with water and gas mains will be part of the purchase price

Further, the water channel surrounding Riffle Rock, will be dredged to a depth of 14 feet to accommodate even the current style of cruisers, and pile-driven breakwater protection will safeguard the island during the worst of storms.

Lots in the million dollar development will be priced from $9,000 to $10,000, and home construction will start in June of 1961. All homes constructed will have all the amenities that quality buyers have come to expect, and will be priced in the $50,000 range.

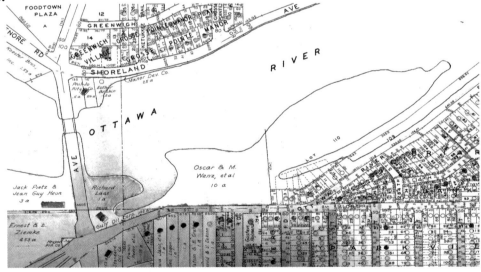

Riffle Rock was to be located in the section of land parallel to the Ottawa River Road and below the word *RIVER* in the map. Courtesy of the Chadwick Lucas County Plat Book 1926.

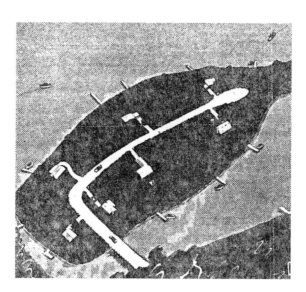

Artist's conception of Riffle Rock. Courtesy of the Toledo Lucas County Public Library.

Current photo of Riffle Rock as it was called in 1960 or more recently Fox's Island. Looking towards I-75 along Ottawa River Road. The Ottawa River would be on the extreme right of the photo. From the author's collection.

Mr. & Mrs. Bill Poupard

".. If it wouldn't have been for Bill and Lillian Poupard and I think a guy named Bill Morgan, I don't know what I would have done," recalls longtime resident and current mayor of Point Place Howard Pinkley. "We were sailing the ice-boat from the Bay into the River and somehow I managed to straddle the ice gorge that always forms, you know, in the mouth of the Ottawa River just off Odeon Island and the Lost Peninsula. I had the horn of the 10 Meter on one side and the rear skate on the other, and the runner plank was just dangling in the open water. I had Sally Hoffman, Cam King's granddaughter with me at the time and she suggested that I walk over to Odeon [Indian] Island and get the Poupards to help us out. She knew the Poupards through her grandfather. Well, at that time the island was pretty good size and I found a path that worked its way through barren trees to their cabin. I explained my predicament and it wasn't long before experienced hands and some long wooden planks had us on our way again."

Howard Pinkley's Ten Meter iceboat is second from the left. Courtesy of Howard Pinkley.

Lillian and her husband Bill Poupard had lived on Odeon or Indian Island as it is known now since 1914, and when they were interviewed in 1934 Lillian said *"oh,*

fishing is pretty hard work, dragging in heavy nets and all, but I wouldn't trade this life for all the card parties and picture shows there are. " Odeon Island was located at the mouth of the Ottawa River and was one of a string of islands that you would encounter on your way to Bay Point or Woodtick Peninsula. Squaw Island and Gard Island were the other two.

Lillian and Bill Poupard on Odeon Island 1934. Courtesy of John Robinson Block and the Toledo BLADE.

The Poupards' lived in a cabin nestled among a large grove of trees that grew on the island, and seined for fish throughout the fall into the early winter. *".. People think the winters out here would be bad, but we don't mind them. We bring out plenty of coal and groceries, and we have a radio. We get along fine. There seems to be a lot of trouble going on in the world, but it doesn't seem to bother us out here,"* said Mrs Poupard to Virginia Nelson a BLADE reporter who visited them in August of 1934. Lillian's husband Bill was of French descent and didn't say too much to the reporter. While Lillian was talking to the reporter, Bill enjoyed the pleasant afternoon sitting in the shade of a willow tree, playing the harmonica, while he repaired several fishing nets that were drying in the sun.

Othedus and Hilda Campbell

Their neighbors never complained, and during the summer months of 1958 their music could be heard throughout the neighborhood surrounding Edgewater School. The Campbells had one of the largest theater pipe organs in the tri-state area. Located in their guest house on 133rd Street, the residence was remodeled to accommodate the growth of the pipe organ. Living next door helped, but the Campbell's were spending most of their free time traveling throughout the country looking for parts to refurbish their organ.

Garrett Avenue or 133rd Street in Point Place looking towards Edgewater Drive circa 1920. Courtesy of Ella Kriener.

133rd Street as it appeared in 2006. From the author's collection.

The Campbell's decided to build the pipe organ in 1951 after losing interest in short wave radio broadcasting. Some of the 1,082 pipes of various sizes came from the Presbyterian Church in Tecumseh, Michigan, and some of those pipes were salvaged from the Pantheon Theater on St. Clair Street here in Toledo. Another set of pipes came from St. John's Church in Williston, Ohio, while still others came from Illinois and Indiana.

To install the keyboard inside the guest house the exterior wall had to be removed to accommodate the three levels of keyboards that came from a theater in Camden, New Jersey. Once the keyboard was installed in the living room, extensive remodeling was required to accommodate the beautiful woodwork of the keyboards along with the 95 stops or buttons. It's not unusual to hear various bird whistles, car horns, thunder, fire sirens, and most musical instruments coming from the guest house.

The home on Garrett Street was remodeled to accommodate the pipe organ. From the author's collection.

While the pipe organ is capable of playing, Mr. Campbell said that with over 30,000 soldered connections in the miles of electrical wiring needed to connect the various parts the organ won't be complete until some time in 1959.

John and Ella Hart

Bound in the original goatskin, the Harts of Point Place had in their library *Luther's Doctrines.* The book was printed in Strassburg, Germany in 1601, and passed from one generation of the Harts to the next. Various owners starting with Ludovius Kodig in 1695, including one of Hart's ancestors in 1825, wrote that they were the sole owner of *Luther's Doctrines.*

Containing more than 700 pages with wood cuts to match, book worms, children, and even vandals have visited destruction upon the book. Funny faces obviously drawn by children are on page three, and pages 201 to 207 have been cut out of the book.

John Hart and *Luther's Doctrines* from the Toledo TIMES of 1930. Courtesy of John Robinson Block and the Toledo BLADE.

According to John Hart, *"I've sent photographs of the title pages of* Luther's Doctrines *to some of the largest libraries in the world, and all of them had never seen or heard of another volume like it. It gets its value from its age and the fact that it contains accurate history that cannot be found elsewhere."*

The Benore Road Underpass

Located on Benore Road approximately where Alexis Avenue and Benore Road now intersect stood the Benore Road underpass for the Michigan Central Rail Road freight yard. Initially, Alexis Avenue originally stopped at Detroit Avenue and wasn't extended to Suder Avenue till 1972. Without the convenience of I-75 the two main thoroughfares from the Point – Shoreland area to West Toledo were Matzinger and Benore.

Pee Wee's Inn at Suder Avenue and Benore Road. Circa 1950. Courtesy of the Point Place Heritage Society.

Entrance to PeeWee's Inn, circa 1930. Courtesy of Nancy Stoddard.

Shore Line Café at Benore Road and the DT&SL Railroad tracks. Courtesy of the Point Place Heritage Society.

Turning left [west] onto Benore Road off Suder you went past Pee Wee's Inn on your left, and in about 300 feet or the length of a football field, Matzinger Road followed the course of the Ottawa River to the left, and Benore went northwest. At the intersection of Benore and the Detroit Toledo & ShoreLine railroad tracks was the Shore Line Café. Your drive to West Toledo on either Matzinger or Benore was frequently interrupted by the continuously traveled railroad tracks.

Looking north; Suder Avenue runs top to bottom on the right, the intersection is Shoreland, the Detroit Toledo and ShoreLine Railroad runs top to bottom on the left, Benore Road runs from lower right to upper left, and Matzinger leaves Benore Road on the left middle. Circa 1956. Courtesy of the Abrams Aerial Survey Corporation, City of Toledo, Engineering Division.

To alleviate part of the problem with the railroads on Benore Road the Michigan Central Railroad built an overpass over Benore for their yard where Waste Management has their landfill. Starting at approximately Hallet Tower on Matzinger Road the Michigan Central line started climbing to gain the height needed for the Benore Road overpass. Once the freight cars passed over the "hump" as it was called it was downhill to one of the selected tracks in the yard.

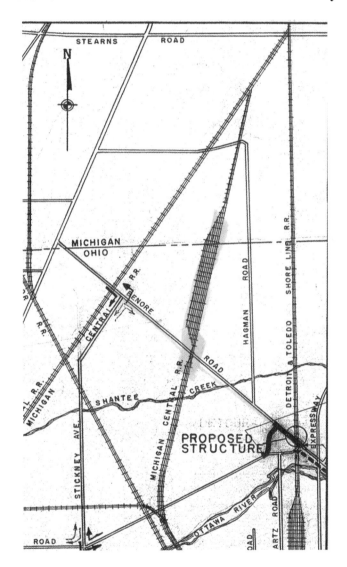

Looking north this drawing shows Benore Road with the MCRR line coming from Hallet Tower [Matzinger Road] over Benore Road into the yard and connecting with the New York Central RR. Circa 1927. State of Ohio, City of Toledo Division of Engineering.

In one of our many conversations about the area, Charlie Stahl told me about the time as a young boy he was fishing on Half-Way Creek near Lotus and Hagman Road.

" We would leave the house on Detroit early to go fishing, and cut the corner to Benore Road where Silver Creek crosses. It was all plowed fields then and easy walking. We would follow Silver Creek till it joined Half Way Creek at the end of the Michigan Central Rail Yard. Now, it would be at about Lotus Drive and Hagman Road, on the other side of Waste Management's landfill. The fishing was real good by the train bridges, and hobo's used the same area to camp. They had pretty good shelter under the railroad bridges and they could catch freights from there heading to all parts of the country. We carried our worms in a coffee can and one of the hobos kept looking in our direction. I wasn't very old then and I asked my older brother about the guy that kept looking at us. Ah, he said, they won't hurt us. Finally the guy comes over and asks if he could have our fairly new worm can in exchange for his old rusty one. He said that he boiled coffee in his can and that the coffee was starting to taste like the can, but our new coffee can …. Well, we dumped our worms into his can, and we gave him our worm can. As the hobo walked back to his campfire he stopped by the edge of the stream and filled his new possession with water for the morning's coffee. It wasn't till many years later that my brother and I learned that we had met Maury "Steam Train" Graham, King of the Hobos."

Randy Stahl with Maury "Steam Train" Graham at Metcalf Field 1980. Courtesy of Charles and Katherine Stahl.

The King family were living on a farm during the Depression just west of the Michigan Central Railroad yard and north of Benore Road and they remember the back ground noise of the railroad cars as the yard engines made them into workable trains.

Albert and Marie King in the front yard of their farmhouse on Benore Road. Circa 1939 or 1940. Courtesy of Gene and Marcia King.

Lois Bennett and Doug King in 1934. Notice the line of freight cars in the background. Courtesy of Gene and Marcia King.

Bernard and Mary Lou King. In the extreme right of the background the Benore Road underpass is just visible. Circa 1934. Courtesy of Gene and Marcia King.

The Benore Road underpass for the Michigan Central Railroad yard, looking east towards Point Place. Circa 1934. Courtesy of Gene and Marcia King.

Today the Benore Road underpass would have been approximately located at the intersection of Benore Road and Alexis, and was removed sometime in the late 1960's or 1970's about the same time as Alexis Road was extended from Detroit Avenue to Suder Avenue.

**Washington Township Constables
or Police Protection in
Point Place**

Constable Joe Marleau 1935.
Courtesy of Richard Marleau.

Deputy Sheriff Marvin Pedee. Circa
1910. Courtesy of Larry Pedee.

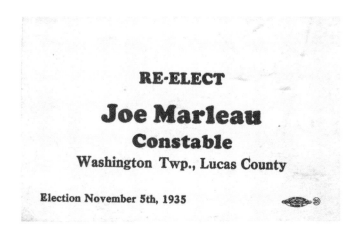

Re-elect Joe Marleau Washington Township. Courtesy of Richard Marleau.

Constable Joe Marleau on Shoreland Avenue in 1935. Courtesy of Richard
Marleau.

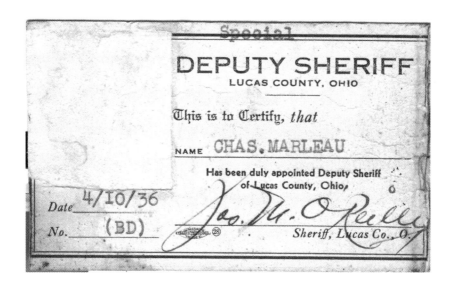

Special Deputy Sheriff Charles Marleau 1936 issued from Lucas County Sheriff
O'Reilly. Courtesy of Richard Marleau.

 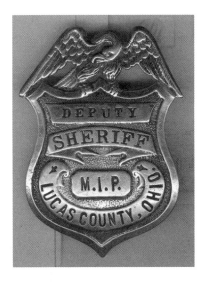

Marvin Pedee helped to enforce the laws in Point Place's Washington Township. Courtesy of his son, Larry Pedee.

Police firing range Bay View Park at the south end of Detwiler Marsh. Courtesy of the Toledo Lucas County Public Library.

Fire Protection in Point Place

Point Place Fire Station Number One dedicated May 7, 1923. The station was located at Seal [115ᵗʰ Street] and Summit Streets. Courtesy of the Point Place Heritage Society.

Fire protection for Point Place was sketchy at best, and when the City of Toledo passed an ordinance requiring that people having residences outside the city limits would pay so much an hour for active fire-fighting it was the last straw. Washington Township formed the West Bay Shore Improvement Association to guide the residents towards their own fire department in November of 1922. With 27 trained volunteer fireman and $5,000 invested in equipment The Point Place or Washington Township Fire Department became operational on May 7, 1923. From that date on the Point Place resident's always said that their volunteer fire department was the best in Ohio.

Seated in front of the fire truck from l-r: L. Klaiber, Gus Cummerow, C. A. Kleis, and Dr. Barney Hein, department surgeon. Standing in front of the fire truck [2nd row] from l-r: James McClelland, George Stader, Henry Eikost, Frank Curson, Fred Kolling, Chief Baertschi, Edward Blessman, Earl Jordan, Norton Pinkley, Ernest Hochstetter, and Arthur Hilt. Standing on the fire truck [3rd row] from l-r: Theodore Vilhaurer, Robert Haines, George Launders, Michael Stader, Otto Hesse, Walter Torgler, Richard Remely, and Fred Kleis. The Point Place Volunteer Fire Department on May 20, 1924. It should be noted that Chief Baertschi had over twenty five years service with the Toledo Fire Department at Station 12 on Summit Street. Courtesy of Howard Pinkley

Today, residents of Point Place report a fire by dialing *911*, but in 1924 the system was a bit more involved. Using the telephone you would ask for the operator of the *Edgewater Exchange* and report the fire. The operator would take your name and the location of the conflagration. The operator would then call C. A. Kleis, secretary of the fire board, and relay the information. Mr. Kleis would then press a button near his telephone which would sound the two large sirens on either side of the fire station. Hearing the alarm sound the volunteer firemen would rush to the fire station, assemble and gather their equipment, and then rush to the fire's location.

When Point Place came into the City of Toledo residents could report a fire in a couple of ways. You could call the operator who would report the fire, or you could use one of the sixteen call boxes that were located throughout the Point.

Call Box Locations

1411	**Naval Armory**
1412	**101st Street and Summit Street**
1413	**108th Street and Summit Street**
1414	**114th Street and Summit Street**
1415	**123rd Street and Summit Street**
1416	**126th Street and Summit Street**
1417	**Unknown**
1418	**109th Street and 301st Street**
1419	**United States Coast Guard**
1420	**Unknown**
1421	**116th Street and 291st Street**
1422	**113th Street and 296th Street**
1423	**119th Street and 297th Street**
1424	**104th Street and 290th Street**
1425	**Lehman Avenue and 290th Street**
1426	**108th Street and 287th Street**
1427	**Lehman Avenue and Onandaga Avenue**
1428	**Lehman Avenue and Suder Avenue**
1429	**Ottawa River Road and 108th Street**
1430	**Unknown**
1431	**117th Street and 304th Street**
1432	**121st Street and 304th Street**
1433	**125th Street and 309th Street**
1434	**131st Street and 304th Street**
1435	**Edgewater Drive and 131st Street**
1436	**Edgewater Drive and 135th Street**
1437	**Lakeside and 138th Street**
1438	**Edgewater Drive and 140th Street**
1439	**Lakeside Drive and 141st Street**
1440	**Unknown**
1441	**Edgewater Drive and 145th Street**
1442	**Lakeside Drive and 145th Street**
1443	**Edgewater Drive and 149th Street**

An example of the records that were kept when Point Place came under Toledo's umbrella of fire protection from Station 24's Logbook.

Fire   Saturday, August 4th, 1945
Still Box 1438 at 9:50 am in 10:10 am, no work, Fire at 5821 Edgewater Drive, owner George Erd, occupant Eli Suzor. Piers broke letting building drop in creek, breaking

meter and box from building, short circuiting electrical wires outside of building. Fire out on arrival. No work. Absent 20 minutes.

Fire   Thursday, May 9th, 1946
Alarm Box 1436 @ 9:17 am. All in 11:21 am #24 in at 11:21. 20' ladder 1 booster 600' of hose. Worked 2 hrs 4 min. Reported hydrant works hard.

Fire   Wednesday, January 19th, 1949
Alarm Box 1434 @ 12:35 pm # 24 Pumper 12:47 pm auto fire 131st Street and 303rd Street, no damage, no work, H. Badman 20 Edgewater Park. Cause anti-freeze, no work.

Point Place Volunteer Fire Department 19. Those shown in the picture are: C. E. McClellan, Gustavus Cummerow, Louis Klaiber commissioner, John Durand secretary, Walter Torgler chief, Charles Winzeler first assistant, Henry Eikost, Ted Villhauer, Ernest Fuchs, Kenneth Mouery, Thomas Swinghammer, Robert Lees, Clarence Saas, Robert McDowell, Harold Pinkley, Ralph Gray, Junius Riker, Eddie Lawler, and Howard Kleis. Members not in the picture: Walter Vance, Robert Hayner, Fred Drogmiller, Harry Hoose, Irvin Lentz, Russel Kern, Glen Dreery, Paul Blum, Edward Blessman, Ernest Hockstetter, Cecil Ellis, and Dr. H. W. Williamson. Courtesy of the Toledo Lucas County Public Library.

Cafes & Bars & Saloons

Alice & Rays

Alice and Ray's

WATER FRONT BAR

The Bar Over the Water

5827 Edgewater Drive

⚓

We Specialize in

— FINE FOODS —

Anything can happen here

and usually does

⚓

BEER — WINE

PO. 0223

**Interior of Alice and Rays. Circa 1949.
Al Martin, Larry Voltz, Roy Kern.
Courtesy of Nancy Stoddard.**

May 17, 1949
41-5 Fire Alarm Box 1436 @ 9:13 pm   return 3:20 am   worked: 6 hrs 7 mins
41-6 Special Alarm Box 1436 @ 9:29 pm Nos 1-13 Pumpers
*   1000 ft of hose 40ft ladder 1 booster*

The above information was courtesy of Ralph Emory and the Toledo Fire Museum.

The above is the official fire log notation of Toledo Fire Station No.24 in response to the two alarm fire at Mrs. Arthur M. Totzke's Water Front Bar at 5827 Edgewater Drive. When 24's pumper arrived on the scene the building was completely engulfed in flames, and a "special" alarm was called in. Four pumpers responded; 24's, 19's, 1's, and 13's. The Hook & Ladder from 1's and the rescue squad from 3's. All told their were six pieces of equipment and over twenty fire fighters that responded to the second alarm at Alice & Ray's.

The Water Front Bar burned to the ground with a complete loss, and the two apartments upstairs were also destroyed. Gladys Fink and Mrs. Bernice Knoppe estimated their combined loss at $3500. The saloon's estimated loss was in excess of $12,000, and with televisions just coming on the market the examiner wrote *"Television set owned by Martin bar tender insurance loss not covered in excess of $250 on set."*

Nicknamed the "Bloody Bucket," Point Place resident Jim Reno remembers the fire. *"I was six years old at the time and I remember hearing the sirens. As they got closer to the house, we lived on 138th Street, my brother and I looked out the back window and the flames were reflected along the whole waterfront. The river [Ottawa] looked like it was alive. We sat on the back steps and watched it burn to the ground. No matter what the firemen did … it burned down.*

"After Alice & Ray's burned down," recalls another Point Placer, *"A bunch of us kids spent the next day hunting for the dimes that were in the shuffleboard's coin box. Never did find it. Maybe someone else got there before I did. Sometimes when I was poking around in the burned wood the flames would start up again from the ashes. Boy, my feet got hot. Never did tell my Mother."*

This aerial view of the Ottawa River is the only photo of Alice & Ray's that I have been able to locate. The Waterfront Bar is the white building with the wide veranda porch located in the upper left center of the photo. Courtesy of the Point Place Heritage Society.

Turtle Club

Café located off Gard Island in 1931, a forerunner of the Turtle Club. Courtesy of
the Toledo *NEWS-BEE*

As the approaching thunder storm swept across the Maumee Bay, Russ Kisseberth's
fishing party sought shelter in the lee of Turtle Island. Waiting for the storm to blow
itself out Russ remarked *"… Turtle Island should have a place to get sandwiches, a
beer, and some worms,"* and from this often heard remark according to Russ and
June's daughter, Carol Griffin, came the idea for the Turtle Club.

The Turtle Club in either 1958 or 1959. It was towed out to Turtle Island several
times during the boating season, and spent the remainder of the time next to Jake
Erd's. Courtesy of Carol Griffin.

Russ's daughter Carol continues *"... Dad and Mom only had a carryout or bumboat liquor license in those days and while he was out to Turtle Island he would position himself in Ohio, so that when the boaters bought the beer they were in Ohio. When they left, they would cross an imaginary state line into Michigan, where they could legally consume their favorite beverages.*

The Turtle Club tied up next to Jake Erd's Dock in 1961. Courtesy of Carol Griffin.

Inside the Turtle Club. The picture on the left was taken in 1961, and the picture on the right taken in the late 60's has Russ Kisseberth on the left.

The Turtle Club was considered under the control of the Coast Guard, consequently every five years it had to be hauled out of the water to be inspected. Courtesy of Carol Griffin.

After the Turtle Club had passed its inspection the club would be hauled out to Gard Island and Russ would throw a huge party for his customers. Just above the partiers the Turtle Club can be found. Courtesy of Carol Griffin.

Returning to its moorings on Edgewater Drive after a successful party. Courtesy of Carol Griffin.

With its business increasing beyond expectations the Turtle Club was rebuilt several times with a huge deck and mooring facilities on the Ottawa River. Chet Jr., Betty, and Chet Sabin on the walkway to the club from Edgewater Drive. Courtesy of Carol Griffin.

Located on Edgewater Drive just north of 138th Street, the Turtle Club suffered a devastating fire in October of 1974. Courtesy of the Point Place Heritage Society.

The Turtle Club during the winter of 1992, notice all the snowmobiles. Courtesy of Betty Sabin.

According to Carol Griffin only a *"real member in good standing knows the password and the answers to the four riddles required for membership."* Courtesy of Carol Griffin.

Hugh Maybe, Betty Sabin, and Bob Martin, with Chuck Reno behind the bar working. Courtesy of Betty Sabin.

On the back deck of the Turtle Club 1987. From l-r: Frank Surprise, Ron Schupp, Lana Boardman, Jerry Sheckler, row 2 Chuck Reno Jr., Donny Francis, Rosebrock, Russ Kisseberth, 3rd row Chuck Reno and Bob Voltz. Courtesy of Betty Sabin.

Using a clam bucket to rip apart the steel barges that supported the almost 50' by 60' structure, the Paxton Demolition Company removed the last vestiges of the Turtle Club. Closed since 1993, it was a sad day in 1997 when the last hope that the Turtle Club would return vanished into Paxton's waiting trucks. In silence, a few of the Turtle's long time friends raised their beer bottles to Russ and June Kisseberth.

Like the Turtle Club, with its edges frayed, torn, and tattered, only the memories of the Turtle Club remain. Courtesy of Carol Griffin.

just a couple of years ago

and some more Point Place café's & restaurants & bars

B·A·R·G·E I·N·N
4861 SUMMIT ST. — PT. PLACE — PO 0293
Beer - Wine - Liquors
OPEN DAILY AT 6:00 A.M.

Courtesy of the TIDBITS issue from August 1951.

● *The Gateway To Point Place*
On Maumee Bay At The Old Casino
The IRISH TAVERN
4133 Summit Street
POntiac 0258

"Erin Go Bragh," says Jim!
The Famous Funhouse for Fishermen, Sailors, Yachtsmen & Golfers, Too
Beer - Wine - Liquors - Mixed Drinks
"HONEST JIM" McCAFFREY, Prop.

Courtesy of the TIDBITS issue from August 1951.

● BIG SCREEN TELEVISION PROJECTION   NOW, EVERY DAY, AT THE
COOL, COMFORTABLY AIR-CONDITIONED
SHORELINE CAFE
BENORE AN] MATZINGER ROAD ———— STANLEY FANDALL AND PHIL BISHOP, Proprietors
¶ BEER ¶ WINE ¶ LIQUORS
100 Record Juke Box — Nine & A Half Ft. Shufflebowl
SANDWICHES & FRENCH FRYS ● FISH FRY, FRIDAY NITES

Courtesy of the TIDBITS issue from August 1951.

Courtesy of the TIDBITS issue from August 1951.

Courtesy of the TIDBITS issue from August 1951.

**Fred C. Young Bridge
or the Summit Street Bridge
over the Ottawa River**

Toledo Beach Interurban line over the Ottawa River. Notice that the bridge swings open and has a full-time operator. Courtesy of the Point Place Heritage Society.

Toledo Beach Interurban car. Courtesy of Frank Pedee and the Point Place Heritage Society.

The Ottawa River Bridge, the Summit Street extension bridge, or the Fred C. Young Bridge was started in January of 1940, and completed in 1941. Shoreland Avenue is on the left and Point Place is on the right. Taken in 1941 this photograph is excellent in depicting the eastern part of Shoreland. Courtesy of the Toledo Lucas County Public Library.

Proposed Ohio State highway number 577 never took its place as part of the Ohio Michigan transportation system joining Detroit and Toledo. The new route which would act as a connector from north Toledo to the Dixie Highway in Erie, Michigan was always known as the Summit Street extension.

Bentley and Son's Construction Company received the contract in January of 1940 from the state. Bidding $280,747 for the complete bridge a company spokesperson said that the bridge would be finished by September 30th of 1941.

The plans were to let the approaches from the north and south completely settle before building the highway. In reality with the coming war construction and road materials were in demand, thus causing a delay in finishing the bridge.

Approaches being filled in for the Ottawa River Bridge. Courtesy of the Point Place Heritage Society.

Approaches being filled in for the Ottawa River Bridge. Courtesy of the Point Place Heritage Society.

Almost finished. Ottawa River Bridge. Courtesy of the Point Place Heritage Society.

Toledo Yacht Club

Initially the history of the Toledo Yacht Club is intertwined with that of a small island named by the early French inhabitants at the mouth of the Ottawa River. Given the name Gard, which in the French language means to guard against, the original deed dates to August 20, 1827 and was signed by President John Quincy Adams. Abner Morse used the island to house his commercial fishing business and even today evidence of the islands early Indian population can be found along its shores.

Toledo Yacht Club, the Naval Armory, and the lagoon from the air. Circa 1953.
Courtesy of the Toledo Lucas County Public Library.

In 1878 Gard Island was purchased from Mr. Quick who had allowed the sailors to use the island and fish in the channel. The original clubhouse for the Toledo Yacht Club was erected on the high ground of Gard Island. The island at one time comprised 18 acres, and had almost a mile of white sand beach to soothe even the most harried businessman and his brood of sand castle builders. In the spring and fall of the year the duck hunting was an added bonus to the bountiful fishing.

The original clubhouse on Gard Island in 1878 for the Toledo Yacht Club. Courtesy of the Toledo Lucas County Public Library.

With its membership mirroring Toledo's population, the Toledo Yacht Club quickly outgrew its first clubhouse, and within twelve years the second clubhouse was built. The second clubhouse had sleeping rooms on the second floor and a spacious first floor to accommodate their growing membership.

Toledo Yacht Club's second clubhouse on Gard Island in 1890. Courtesy of the Toledo Lucas County Public Library.

With year round access to Gard Island becoming a severe problem for Toledo Yacht Club's growing social calendar, the club sold its property on Gard Island to the Erie Shooting Club. The Erie club was still using the yacht club's headquarters till 1920. Gard Island was used by the Toledo Fish Company in 1895 and by 1895 the Toledo Gard Ice Company was in operation. But, by 1898 the island was rescued from this early industrialization by George H. and Valentine Ketcham when they built their palatial summer homes on Gard. Willis Day, of the Willis Day Storage Company, purchased Gard in 1953 and working in concert with Ottawa River Yacht Club and members of the Toledo Outboard Club, erected a 240 foot dock on steel piles.

The club's activities suffered a severe blow during the Flood of 1883 when many of the member's schooners were either destroyed or damaged. Recovery was extremely slow, and with the merger of Ohio Yacht Club, Toledo Yacht Club changed its corporate title to the Toledo Yachting Association.

Toledo Yacht Club's third clubhouse was located on Presque Isle in 1898. Notice the letters T. Y. and A. on the porch roof. Courtesy of the Toledo Lucas County Public Library.

By 1896 finances and interest were once again responding to yachting activities, and in that year the largest international yachting event was held on the Maumee River. The Canada-VanCedore race for the Canada Cup was held in Toledo. With renewed interest Presque Isle, a popular summertime destination and amusement park, was chosen as the site for the new clubhouse. The PASTIME with its numerous trips a day to Presque Isle solved the accessibility issue.

Moving to its present location in Bay View Park, the fourth Toledo Yacht Club clubhouse opened its doors in 1903 and burned to the ground on February 5, 1906. Courtesy of the Toledo Lucas County Public Library.

Presque Isle was a great location for a clubhouse but its facilities were ill equipped to moor its growing fleet of sailing vessels. Many of the club's members found dockage available at the Riverside Boat House at Riverside Park, and when Bay View Park was completed in anticipation of hosting the Ohio Centennial Celebration members found the lagoon perfect.

The fifth and current clubhouse for the Toledo Yacht Club in 1908. Courtesy of the Toledo Lucas County Public Library.

Sensing the advantages of such a location, a twenty-five year lease was arranged with Toledo's Parks Division, and in 1903 the fourth clubhouse opened its doors located in Bay View Park. One year later the historic name of Toledo Yacht Club was restored. When the club burned to the ground in 1906, the $15,000 insurance settlement was the heart of Commodore John Craig, Jr's fire resistant structure that was rising from the ashes of the old.

Several Memories of the MILL'S RACE
by Point Place resident Jim Davis owner of the *ORANGE CRATE*

My first Mill's Race as an owner was in the mid 60's aboard a wooden 33' "pilot" class sloop that had suffered severe fire damage while it was in winter storage. I spent the next two years rebuilding TAMY and launched her about a week prior to the start of the Mills during a stretch of extremely hot weather. I was worried that her new bottom planking would leak, but the only problem we had was with an engine that would run for ten minutes and quit.

On race day the crew consisted of: my father Keith Davis, John Greiner, Tom Davis, Bob Francis, Paul Carr, and several other people who I don't remember. Sure enough the engine ran fine for 10 minutes and quit. As we got closer to the starting line off Harbor Light we hoisted sails and started the race. A short time later John Greiner came up to me and said "Jim we've got some water down below!" As I went to see for myself I was shocked to see the floor boards floating. My Dad quickly lashed the large brass pump to the galley sink, which in our haste I had forgotten to install, and started pumping. We quickly determined that the water was from the topside seams which had not been wet for two to three years and had dried out leaving gaps, so when the boat heeled over the water just streamed in. The whole situation was pretty troubling – no engine, eight miles from shore, and of course the biggest problem – sinking. After a quick conference we decided to start sailing the race and take turns manning the bilge pump … 45 minutes out of every hour we manned that bilge pump. The race was exciting. We encountered several vicious rain squalls, and during the night the entire boat would be illuminated as the lake freighters would shine their million candle power search lights on us. We finished the race in the early morning hours, still pumping 5-10 minutes every hour, as we sailed the boat to the dock at Put-In-Bay. After the seams swelled the boat never leaked another drop while I owned it.

Another memorable race was in 1973. I was sailing a Pearson 36 with Bob Francis, Kenny Sabin, Tom Davis, John Wasielewski, Paul Carr, and Denny Dieball. The race started with a moderate southwest breeze which after several hours into the race developed into one nasty squall after another. Off of Locust Point we took a knock-down with our "star cut" spinnaker up. As the boat lay on its side the spinnaker filled with water. I considered cutting the spinnaker loose before it could drag the entire boat under. Fortunately, before I could give the order the boat righted, the spinnaker dumped its load of water and quickly filled, and we were off again. We won the race overall.

The ORANGE CRATE off South Bass's lighthouse 1982. Courtesy of Jim Davis.

Later in 1973 I decided to try my hand at boat design and building using a relatively new process called "WEST." The entire crew was involved in one way or another. The new wooden boat was launched on May 24, 1974, and after several weeks of sail testing we thought we were ready to try and defend our previous Mill's victory. We had overlooked reef points in the main in our haste to ready the boat, but we managed to do very well with our large sails. Leading at Colchester Reef, we set a spinnaker, and literally surfed downwind with the big waves nearly dead astern. With Bob Francis steering I think I had just closed my eyes for a short nap when Francis yelled "Jim, you better get up here! I can't steer the boat!" Peering over the transom, we spotted our rudder flat on the surface of the water trailing behind the boat.

The ORANGE CRATE had lost its rudder and the crew frantically worked to get our sails down. Afraid of being overtaken in the night, we headed the boat to the southeast to get off the race course, and anchored several miles later near Middle Sister Island. The next morning we were spotted by a Coast Guard helicopter. A crew member from the chopper held a sign which said "are you ok," to which we all replied "yes." As the chopper pulled away we all looked at one another and quickly decided that we were ok, but we could certainly use some help. The chopper must have been thinking the same thing because he returned with a sign "do you need help?" We all indicated yes. Later my father and brother worried about our prolonged absence had rented a plane and were looking for us. About the same time they located us, Marblehead Coast Guard's 40 footer, was approaching following the course radioed by the chopper. We were towed to Put-In-Bay where all of the docks were underwater.

the Toledo Ice Yacht Club

The recognized window emblem found on many of the member's cars. From the author's collection.

Originally thought to have been founded in 1919 with the merger of King's Ice Yacht Club and a group of winter sailors from Toledo Yacht Club, new research indicates that the Toledo Ice Yacht Club dates back to 1895. R. D. Potter was Commodore when just recently the Constitution and By-Laws were unearthed in an unrelated archived group of material at the Toledo Lucas County Public Library.

The line-up of officers for 1895 was as follows:
> R. D. Potter Commodore, H.R. Hone Vice-Commodore, L. G. Colton Secretary & Treasurer, and W. Coakley Measurer. There were three members of the Regatta Committee, and three members of the Entertainment Committee. George Wilds was the Sergeant at Arms, and E. T. Gertz Surgeon.

Yacht	Owner	Date of Election to Membership
Torpedo	R. D. Potter	1895
Zero	H. R. Hone	1895
Early Grave	W. Coakley	1895
Blizzard	R. P. Mathias	1895
Alert	Charles Norton	1895
Snow Flake	James Hough	1895
Reindeer	C. Mathias	1895
Rogue	John Crafts	1895
Cold Wave	Ezra Wulff	1895
Hoo – Doo	L. G. Colton	1895
Cyclone	F. B. Pritchard	1895

& ten others: E. W. Astel 1895. F. M. Bartlett 1895, B. H. Bortee 1895, F. R. Frey 1895, Charles Hall 1895, Walter Lumbar 1895, H. N. Minuse 1895, J. R. Ruswinckel 1895, W. H. St.John 1895, George Wilds 1895, Ed. Grasser 1895, William Lyons 1895, Frank Heyer 1895, Harry Voute 1895, A. A. Scott 1895, M. W. Ingalls 1895, E. T. Gertz 1896, Charles Stanley 1896, George H. Bradt 1896, F. H. Smith 1896, W. Cramer nd, Charles M. Hall nd, and three others that I can't read.

The Constitution and By-Laws held several interesting surprises.

Article XII Meetings. *There shall be two general meetings held during each season. The season runs from December 1ˢᵗ through April 1ˢᵗ.*

By-Laws. Chapter I. Dues. *The initiation fee shall be one dollar, and the annual dues one dollar. Initiation fee must accompany application for membership.*

Chapter VII. Signals. *The distinguishing signal of the Club shall be a pointed burgee; the device the width two-thirds of its length, the field of blue with a large five pointed star in center.*

Rule II. Classification. *Yachts shall be divided into the following classes: Class A. Measuring over 400 square feet. Class B. Measuring from 300 to 400 square feet. Class C. Measuring from 200 to 300 square feet. Class D. Measuring 200 feet or under.*

This well worn TIYC patch belongs to the author.

Snow Cuts Program Of Ice Boat Races

Because of the heavy snow the ice boat racing program of the Toledo Ice Yacht club on Maumee bay at the King's Yacht club was cut to one race in two classes yesterday. Three races in three classes were scheduled.

Claude Lytel sailing the What Fun won the 15-meter event with Jack Bender's Red Cloud second and Mel Frederick's Spare Time third. The Bullfrog with William Komoni at the tiller took the 10-meter race. The Gosling, piloted by Bender, was second and Bud Miller's Mercury third.

CRESCENT SAILORS WILL HOLD RACES

New Ice Yacht Club to Hold First Club Events.

The new Crescent Ice Yacht Club will hold its first races of the season Saturday and Sunday on Maumee Bay with more than a dozen boats expected to compete.

Courtesy of the Toledo BLADE. January 27, 1941

These two articles might explain some of the confusion as to the names Toledo Ice Yacht Club and King's Yacht Club. Both clubs are mentioned in the article on the left. The one on the right mentions Crescent Ice Yacht Club.

Wild Goose Wins Ice Yacht Race

Wild Goose, skippered by Steve Kreiner, won the free for all race of the Toledo Ice Yacht Club off King's yesterday on Maumee Bay.

Second place in yesterday's event went to the Condor, sailed by George Todd and third place to the Ace of Otis Quigley.

In the race Sunday, Quigley took second place with his Ace while first honors went to George King in the Red Cloud and third honors ot Cliff Rodgers in Miss Maumee.

Weather permitting, races will be held again next Sunday.

Courtesy of the Toledo BLADE. The picture on the right has Willie Kormorny explaining the finer points of scaling a 15 Meter mast to Robbie VanWormer.

SCAMP

Skeeter Fleet

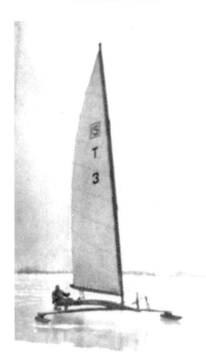

T 77

Redhead T 3

All of the above pictures were copied from the pictures that hung on the wall of Harold King's grocery store on Lakeside Avenue. From the author's collection.

DN 2599. Paul Rossman

DN 1714. Bob Cramer

DN 1977 Bruce Dickson

DN 985 Bob Foeller

All the pictures are from the early 1970's and are from the author's collection.

The 10 Meter Fleet from Toledo Ice Yacht Club. Maumee Bay Circa 1950. From the author's collection.

Archie Call and Renegade 231 coming to the aid of Ken Dickson and his sister-in-law Janet and 15 Meter T34. Courtesy of Jim Stribrny.

From The Toledo Ice Yacht Club News Letter
Feb. 18, 1973

" Kenny Dickson took his sister in law for a ride in hi s
15 Meter on the Maumee Bay -- and went through.

Kenny did manage to explain the reason he went through
the ice was because of a hole -- but Kenny can't or
won't explain why his sister in law got wetter than he
did or how that mysterious foot print got on the middle
of herback. Every man for himself, huh Ken.

Ken and the other sailors on the lake managed to retrieve
his 15-Meter and his sister in law -- probably in that
order to."

**January of 1973. Rescue. From l-r: Ken Dickson, Ron Kolling, Ed Fromme, and
Janet Dickson. Courtesy of Jim Stribrny.**

DN 2564 Jim Reno and Renegade 224 Richard Marleau at the Franklin Park Mall 1973. From the author's collection.

Ken Dickson

Fred Rahtz

Franklin Park Mall 1973. From the author's collection.

Robbie VanWormer and a broken 15 Meter backbone. From the author's collection.

Jack Bernard with a broken runner plank. From the author's collection.

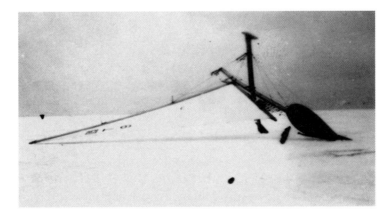

15 Meter T9 on its side Maumee Bay 1935. Courtesy of Charles Dickson.

TIYC old Timer's gathering to tell each other lies. 1974

Lou Klewer and Robbie VanWormer. From the author's collection.

From l-r: Mel Holman, Paul Sweet, Ed Fromme, Doc Bell, Howard Pinkley, Archie Call, Fred Rahtz, unidentified, Fauny Burns, Ron Kolling, Richard Marleau, Jack Hise. Back Row: John Gorun, Ed Bernard, Jack Hugo, and Jim Stribrny. From the author's collection.

From l-r: Ron King, Jack Bernard, Jack Hugo, Ron Kolling, Jim Stribrny, Dick Marleau, Gerry Krouse.

Jim Ickes, Whitey Ickes, Lou Klewer, Frank Ratz

TIYC Historian Jack Hugo.

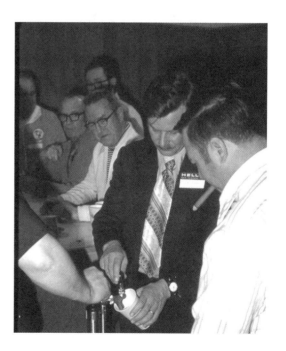

Steve Kreiner, Chet Sabin, John Greiner, Bob Cramer, Pete Biddle.

From l to r: Bob Badman, Dave Voltz, Jack Hugo, and Fred Rahtz. From the author's collection.

Many of the night's stories were told after several beverages. From the author's collection.

Bay View
Yacht Club

BVYC's lagoon before the building of the clubhouse. The Casino, which was built on piers, is located just beyond the spit of land. The old cut is visible in the middle of the photo. Courtesy of James Byrne and the Bay View Yacht Club.

Bay View Yacht Club about 1910 before the peninsula was filled or even thought of. Notice the cut into the bay from the lagoon on the extreme right. Courtesy of James Byrne and the Bay View Yacht Club.

The Toledo Power Boat Club, later to become the Bay View Yacht Club, was the first boating organization on the Great Lakes dedicated to powerboats, with the possible exception, BVYC Historian Jim Byrne says, of a club in Buffalo. The club's first meeting was in the machine shop of boating enthusiast F. M. Underwood on June 1, 1905. With a five dollar initiation fee and dues set at six dollars a year incorporation papers were filed with Ohio's Secretary of State two days later.

For several years the attic of Riverside Boat Club, located on piers in Riverside Park off Summit Street, was home to the financially struggling Toledo Power Boat Club. Four years after Toledo Yacht Club moved to the lagoon in Bay View Park, land was leased at the north end of Bay View's lagoon for dockage and eventually a clubhouse. The main entrance to the lagoon was located near the old sewage plant south of the Naval Armory, and when the Armory was completed in 1935 that entrance was filled. A new entrance to supplement the "old cut" was opened between the Armory and the Coast Guard station. The clubhouse was started in March of 1911 and the annual meeting was held in their completed structure in November of the same year.

Bay View Yacht Club about 1915. Courtesy of Catherine Harms Dice & Neil Hashley and the Point Place Heritage Society.

Looking east, the peninsula is just being constructed and the original entrance into the lagoon Harrison's Marina has been filled. The new cut behind the Naval Armory is in place and operational. The cut by BVYC is still in place. About 1935-1940. Courtesy of James Byrne and the Bay View Yacht Club.

The white building to the left of the middle of the picture is Bay View Yacht Club with Toledo Yacht Club on the lower left and the Naval Armory on the lower right. Courtesy of the Toledo Lucas County Public Library.

Bay View Yacht Club's Ladies Auxiliary 1947. Courtesy of Lucille Ransom and the Point Place Heritage Society.

The clubhouse at Bay View Yacht Club with winter boat storage in the front yard. Courtesy of James Byrne and the Bay View Yacht Club.

In 1922 the club's name was changed to Bay View Yacht Club and they were one of the Associated Yacht Club's charter members. The marine railway was replaced in 1957, and some of the senior club members told of the commercial fishing business with boats and nets that was operated by the Komorny Brothers. The Club's regattas were replaced with the annual homecoming reunion that has become so popular among the Toledo area clubs.

PRESENTS
A WEEK END IN NEW ENGLAND
FEATURING HISTORIC SALEM, MASS.

Bay View Yacht Club's 57th Regatta 1961. Courtesy of James Byrne and the Bay View Yacht Club.

"It would not be possible to mention each individual project or to give recognition to the numerous members who gave unselfishly of their time and of their money to build this facility. Both the club and its present day members owe so much to the men who guided our club toward its present day stature, through good times and bad, through war and peace, through prosperity and depression. They had the Club firmly on its course. … We salute their remarkable efforts." **Jim Byrne, Bay View Yacht Club's Historian.**

Ottawa River Yacht Club

Ottawa River Yacht Club from about 1910. ORYC is located in the very center of the picture. Courtesy of the Point Place Heritage Society.

With just eighty-four feet of water frontage on the Ottawa River, the Ottawa River Yacht Club was started by a hardy group of working men from the Point and surrounding area. Located on Edgewater Drive, the club's first meeting took place in the Spring of 1910, and by the Fall when they received their charter there were 121 members. Dues were three dollars a year.

Ottawa River Yacht Club circa 1915. Courtesy of Ken Levin.

The first couple of years were extremely hard on the club's treasury. Even with all the volunteer help in constructing the docks by 1912 Ottawa River's dues had doubled ---- to six dollars. Ottawa River's first hoist was actually a marine railroad with a cradle attached to a car that would winch a boat in and out of the water. Howard Pinkley recalls, *".. it took about 100 turns on the winch handle to raise the boat about 1 foot .."* According to some early recollections some of the boats were so heavy that the hand winch was attached to the Point Place interurban car. "Jake" Erd would secure one end of the cable to the interurban car and a snatch block was attached to a telephone pole close by and as the street car slowly passed in front of the clubhouse the boat was pulled up the incline of the marine railroad. Old-timers thought that real progress was being made when the marine railway was replaced with a three-legged hoist mounted alongside the bulkhead.

Ottawa River Yacht Club's boat hoist circa 1940. Courtesy of Ida Raker and the Point Place Heritage Society.

With all of the club's money and assets already spent on improvements to the facilities the unemployment of the Depression severely crippled Ottawa River Yacht

Club. Financially brought to its knees, the club's membership dropped to just a few of the officers, and by 1941 there was just $3.80 left in the club's coffee can.

Ottawa River Yacht Club outboard motor races on the Ottawa River circa 1935. Clubhouse on the right and racing boats lined up on the dock. Courtesy of Betty Sabin.

One of the boats involved in the Ottawa River races. The shack on the water is George "Jake" Erd's place. Courtesy of the Point Place Heritage Society.

The ORYC crew driving sheet metal retaining wall in 1950. From l – r: Park Hefenger, Jake Erd, Larry Voltz, Chet Sabin, Frank Rate, and Ed McNutt. Courtesy of Larry Voltz and the Point Place Heritage Society.

Same job different crew at ORYC in 1950. From l – r: Ralph Lashaway, Park Hefenger, Larry Voltz, Jake Erd, Ed McNutt, and Chet Sabin standing on the rig. Courtesy of Larry Voltz and the Point Place Heritage Society.

Ottawa River Yacht Club Regatta brochure 1947. From the author's collection.

Nipper Class sailboats on the Ottawa River for the Ottawa River Yacht Club 1947 Regatta. Courtesy of the Point Place Heritage Society.

**Lightning Class sailboats on the Ottawa River for the Ottawa River Yacht Club
1947 Regatta. Courtesy of the Point Place Heritage Society.**

**Ottawa River Yacht Club's *"T"* dock just after World War II. Courtesy of the Point
Place Heritage Society.**

The Leudtke 22' Cat Boat Fleet racing on the Ottawa River in 1961. Notice the Summit Street Bridge in the background on the left. Courtesy of Howard Pinkley.

Future member of ORYC on the main dock in 1952. Courtesy of Larry Voltz and the Point Place Heritage Society.

Jolly Roger Sailing Club

Coming out of World War II when boys of 16 were forced to assume the roles of young adults, eight Point Place sailors, who had been racing Nippers for years on the Ottawa River, gathered together to talk about sailing in Bud's garage on 145th Street. Ed Schweitzler, Bud's father, said that the boys could use the family's old chicken coup in the back of their property near the lagoon for future meetings.

In the Summer of 1946 Ronnie Anderson, Dick Gibbs, Bud Schweitzler, Dick and Cleon Reckly, Chuck Fuller, Joe Haselbeck, and Stan Kelly spent the next couple of days cleaning and white-washing the chicken coup. When they finished the coup was so small that only Commodore Dick Gibbs and several of his officers were able to fit inside, the other five members of the future Jolly Roger Sailing Club had to stick their heads through the windows to attend the meetings.

Pooling their money, the eight young sailors decided to build a clubhouse behind Schweitzler's garage. Salvaging what they could from the chicken coup and scrounging the Point for the rest of the building materials Jolly Roger Sailing Club's second clubhouse began to take shape.

Jolly Roger Sailing Club clubhouse behind Ed Schweitzler's garage. Circa 1946. Courtesy of Bob Fox and the Jolly Roger Sailing Club.

With no access to the Ottawa River from the lagoon which ran parallel to 146ᵗʰ Street the next project was to locate a suitable piece of property from which they could launch and dock their sailboats. Ed Hughes who owned the half finished house at 5956 Edgewater Drive said that he would sell the boys his waterfront on Edgewater. Located south of Komorny's Fish Market [5971 Edgewater Drive], piles were driven in the river to expand the property and the filling was underway.

This picture shows Edgewater Drive before the Jolly Roger Sailing Club or the Toledo Outboard Club [River View Yacht Club] had their facilities on the Ottawa River. On the extreme middle left is the bridge which allowed access to the lagoon. Next, the little white building is the pump house at Edgewater and 145ᵗʰ Street. The large white building on the right is Komorny's Fish Market and the property to the right was the future home of the Jolly Roger Sailing Club. The sailboat is of course a *Nipper.* Circa 1947. Courtesy of Bob Fox and the Jolly Roger Sailing Club.

With the land purchased for the clubhouse the boys contacted Ottawa River Yacht Club. A deal was soon struck, and Chet Sabin agreed to drive the piles for the wharf's bulkhead in exchange for the boys painting Ottawa River Yacht Club's clubhouse. With none of the proper permits required, Jolly Roger Sailing Club made their plans to move their clubhouse from 146ᵗʰ Street to the Ottawa River.

At this point there is disagreement between the early members as to what actually happened. One theory is that after the boys had carefully lifted the garage structure off its concrete block piers, Manuel Casey backed his trailer under the braced clubhouse and headed for the bulkhead filled wharf. Once they reached Edgewater Drive the garage slid off the trailer and completely blocked the flow of traffic in and out of the Point. When the police arrived they looked the situation over and ordered that all the spectators gather around the garage, pick it up, and place the structure back on the trailer. And according to Bob Fox that's what happened. On the other hand John Greiner said that the clubhouse was placed on steel pipe and rolled towards its new home. The steel pipes were dragged from the rear and placed in the front to begin the process all over again. Since both of these men are honorable and not prone to exaggeration they must have viewed the event from different vantage points. Either way with the tedious move completed the next step was to position the clubhouse on its new pier foundation overlooking the Ottawa River.

**Jolly Roger Sailing Club at its new location on the Ottawa River. Circa 1952.
Courtesy of Bob Fox and the Jolly Roger Sailing Club.**

The wharf, clubhouse, and launching dock. Courtesy of Bob Fox and the Jolly Roger Sailing Club.

Telephone poles were used to reinforce the wharf's bulkheads, and by the mid 1950's most of the club's construction were finished. Chet Sabin, of the Ottawa River Yacht Club, was probably one of the most helpful non-sailors the club ever had. Without money for cars let alone trailers the club's early members were towed from one yacht club regatta to another behind Chet's power boat.

According to Jolly Roger Sailing Club's unwritten history even the Coast Guard would help out on occasion. Senior members swore an oath that the Toledo built ice-breaker the *MACKINAC* had at one time placed the club's sailboats on its deck and delivered them to Put-In-Bay for the Inter Lake Yachting Association races.

By 1960 Jolly Roger Sailing Club had outgrown its small garage clubhouse and Mr. Hughes' unfinished basement property across the street looked perfect for the planned expansion.. Condemned by the City of Toledo and with the purchase price negotiated with Mr. Hughes', Jolly Roger Sailing Club completed its new clubhouse on the rebuilt foundation at 5960 Edgewater Drive. Large enough for 70 members the new clubhouse served its members for almost twenty years. In 1978 a huge expansion guided by club members was added to the rear of the clubhouse and additional property including Johnson's cherry orchard was added to accommodate the club's growing membership.

The Jolly Roger Sailing Club in 1961. Courtesy of Bob Fox and the Jolly Roger Sailing Club.

Jolly Roger Sailing Club's floating docks. Circa 1958. Courtesy of Bob Fox and the Jolly Roger Sailing Club.

True to their commitment to foster the next generation of sailors, new junior members Ben and Les Lashaway, to meet their membership requirements, painted the picket fence in front of the clubhouse. **Courtesy of Bob Fox and the Jolly Roger Sailing Club.**

Jolly Roger Sailing Club is on the left of the photo, the Toledo Outboard Club's clubhouse is on right. Notice the bulkhead in the forefront. **Courtesy of Bob Fox and Jolly Roger Sailing Club.**

Picture taken at an unknown location in July of 1949.

Awards from July of 1949. 1ˢᵗ row from l-r: Howard Pinkley, Joe Haselbeck, Cleon Reckley, Rod Erwin, Paul Hughes, Roger Erwin, Cecil O'Connel. 2ⁿᵈ Row: Chuck Fuller, Gary Gordon, Ron Anderson [sort of standing], Dick Quinlan, Don Hoyt, Ben Barber, Don Pinkley, Virgil Hughes. 3ʳᵈ Row: unknown with hat, unknown young lady, Dick Milinck, Roman Ludwick, Jim Reno, Sonny Audry. Courtesy of Bob Fox and the Jolly Roger Sailing Club.

Same awards ceremony. Courtesy of Howard Pinkley.

River View Yacht Club
Toledo Outboard Club

Al Perkins and hydroplane racing on the Ottawa River. Courtesy of Al Antoine and River View Yacht Club.

After several great summers of hydroplane racing on the Ottawa River after World War II, the racers found themselves meeting informally to plan the next round of races. In November of 1949 with Al Perkins of 138th Street leading the way, this small group of enthusiasts met at Bob Fisher's Outboard Marine Repair on Edgewater Drive, to see if there was enough interest to form a club devoted to outboards.

Al Perkins, one of the founders of the Toledo Outboard Club. Courtesy of River View Yacht Club.

Bob Fisher's Outboard Marine Repair shop on Edgewater Drive. Circa 1954. Courtesy of the Toledo Lucas County Public Library.

With the help of outdoor BLADE writer and boating enthusiast Lou Klewer a second meeting was held at Bob Fisher's place on November 22, 1949, and the twenty-two men present elected Al Perkins as their representative. With Al Perkins leading the way the Toledo Outboard Club was organized in January of 1950. The membership of the Toledo Outboard Club quickly outgrew Fisher's cramped quarters and as winter turned to spring they found themselves meeting at Thompson's Inn.

**The Toledo Outboard Club's fleet docked at Thompson's Inn. Circa 1950 0r 1951.
Courtesy of Al Antoine and River View Yacht Club.**

Construction was started on grounds of the present clubhouse in the spring of 1951 and with plenty of volunteer labor from the membership roster of 32 the original clubhouse was open for business in November of 51. The first floating docks were in place by the Spring of 52 and by 1959 they had all been replaced by permanent docks. Commodore Don Ritnour guided the expansion to the original clubhouse in the Spring of 1955 and watched over its completion one year later. The club's original land footprint was expanded to the west under Commodore Fry, and later expanded again to include Louie's docks and hoist to the north, and boat storage area to the east.

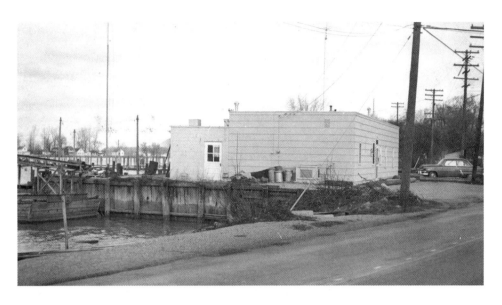

The Toledo Outboard Club in the Fall of 1955 with the expansion completed before the winter snows fell. Note the pile driver in the extreme left of the photo that was built by the club members, and the narrow Edgewater Drive. Courtesy of Al Antoine and River View Yacht Club.

River View Yacht Club's floating docks. Circa 1953 to 1958. Courtesy of Al Antoine and River View Yacht Club.

TOLEDO OUTBOARD CLUB

1st Annual REGATTA

10th ANNIVERSARY CELEBRATION

A Y C *Sponsored*

SATURDAY and SUNDAY

AUGUST 15, 16 1959

5981 Edgewater Dr.

River View Yacht Club's 1st Annual Regatta was held in August of 1959. Courtesy of Al Antoine and River View Yacht Club.

The early seventies again brought change to the Toledo Outboard Club. The club's name was changed to River View Yacht Club and even the darkening mood swings of Lake Erie couldn't curb the enthusiasm that was taking the club to new heights.

The severe floods of November of 1972 and April of 1973 brought not only severe damage to the clubhouse, but the flood's receding waters brought *Operation Foresight* to Point Place. With the City of Toledo's budget already strapped, the Army's Corps of Engineer's eight foot high pre-fabricated rock boxes ringed with chain-link fence provided *"a one size fits all"* solution to the Point's water problems. While solving the flooding problem in the short term, the rock boxes brought to the club new obstacles with regards to dock and hoist access.

Looking west from the north end of Edgewater Park in April of 1973. From the author's collection.

Low water at River View Yacht Club. From the author's collection.

Couple flood protection with the recurring bouts of low water in the Ottawa River basin, River View Yacht Club could have been in serious difficulty if not for the tenacity and resolve of its membership. River View Yacht Club not only survived, but prospered into the coming years.

IRVING SCHAUB MEMORIAL RACE
September 9, 1951
Courtesy of *Along the WaterFront   Jake Erd   TIDBITS*

● Two pilots flipped their fast outboards over at the 20 mile marathon Irving Schaub Memorial Race Sunday, Sept. 9th on Ottawa River. It was one of the roughest course races the Toledo Outboard Club has ever run. The two dunked skippers were **Norm Romstadt** and **Bob Lally** of McClure, Ohio. This race was for members only. Winners were first place, **Bob Shull**, second, **Ralph Kachenmeister** and third, **Bill Apel**. The T. O. B. C. will hold another race on Sept. 23rd at 1 p.m. Walbridge Park. First, second and third place trophies. A-B-C St. Utility. A-B-C St. Hydro 1 heat 5 laps, open to all.

The Toledo Outboard Club membership is still open to any skipper who has his own outboard. It's their rule every member must own a boat.

Betty [Deeds] PERKINS
describes the murder of Jack Kennedy
Courtesy of the Point Place Herald and the Point Place Heritage Society.

At the present time my husband Alvin Perkins and I have been residents of Point Place for 45 years, but in the early 1900s my father, Ralph G. Deeds, and our family spent every summer in Point Place. …

In the beginning, our family owned a cottage on the water on Edgewater Drive across from the Moose Lodge [now Bush Marine]. However, the water frequently rose and we were forced to wade around on the first floor. …. A bargain came along in a house next door to Ottawa River Yacht Club. … We also found out that our house had previous owners who were bootleggers as we were awakened at night by people wanting booze. ….

One dark evening in July, 1933 at about 9:30 pm … we were sitting on our porch when along came Jack Kennedy and a lady friend walking hand in hand. …. Immediately after they walked past our house a car with some men in it stopped in front of our house. …. My father thought the men were coming to see him from the Eagles. … The car then proceeded slowly down the road. …. They shot Kennedy, got back in the car, turned around and sped down Edgewater. … My father shouted "Get their license number." Curiosity got the best of me and over the objections of my mother and dad, I ran to the corner to see what was happening. I was about 13 years old at the time.

Mudjaw Bowmen

The club's emblem was designed by Howie Lang and is recognized throughout the tri-state area as belonging to the Mudjaw Bowmen of Toledo, Ohio. Courtesy of the Mudjaw Bowmen and John Sinkovic.

Dues were in 1953 three dollars a year and on the 1st and 3rd Thursday of each month the Town Tavern was the Mudjaw Bowmen's first clubhouse. According to the club's written history Edward VanderHorst was elected the club's first president, and the first sanctioned shoot was held in March of 1953 behind the Coast Guard property in Point Place.

Angelo's Spaghetti House on Stickney Avenue was the site of the club's first annual banquet and signaled the opening of the outdoor range in Detwiler Marsh [Detwiler Golf Course] off Lehman and 290th Street near the Hill Top Stables. Some members recall having an archery range set up in the basement of one of downtown Toledo's landmark buildings. The truth of the matter may belong to the upper floors of the Sanford Pet Shop at 126 Summit Street where the club had set up an indoor range during the winter months of 1954. By late 1954 the club had once again moved to its new outdoor range on Benore Road across from the old gambling buildings.

The "old" clubhouse on the Benore Road property just east of the Michigan Central Railroad "hump." Many of the individual archery ranges were back stopped by the railroad's roadbed. If you look closely to the left of the clubhouse the white gambling buildings on Benore Road are just visible. Courtesy of the Mudjaw Bowmen and John Sinkovic.

With the local, state, and federal law enforcement agencies cracking down on organized gambling it wasn't long before game's of chance disappeared from Washington Township and Benore Road. Long time Mudjaw Bowmen member Howie Lang describes how the club got the property on Benore.

"… When the club first located on Benore Road – An abandoned gambling casino was located on the south side of the road. We envisioned an indoor range and check house. One member, Bud Wilson, knew who to ask for permission to rent, lease or use the building. Enter "Chalky Red" Yaronowsky. …. He allowed Mudjaw Bowmen to use the building rent free, if we maintained the facility. This was the indoor range for many years until the present building was built."

The "Benore Club" building that was used by the Mudjaw Bowmen for an indoor archery range. Circa 1970. Courtesy of the Mudjaw Bowmen and John Sinkovic.

The Mudjaw Bowmen Benore Road Sign. Courtesy of the Mudjaw Bowmen and John Sinkovic.

In 1965 property for an outdoor range became available. Located east of the State Line Cemetery the 30 acres straddled the Ohio Michigan State Line and had access

off Benore Road. Once again Mudjaw Bowmen member Howie Lang describes how the club got the present property on Benore.

"…. Along about the mid sixties the present property was for sale. When we contacted the sellers, we discovered that a group from Detroit was the owner and "Chalky Red" was again contacted and the purchase price negotiations were begun. Mudjaw, not having much, if any, money was the recipient of financial assistance, the loan was arranged by the Detroit group. After the purchase the archery range construction was begun. The need for construction equipment, earth movers and bulldozers, was arranged working through "Chalky Red." We were allowed to use this equipment from the Jechura Brothers, owners of Raceway Park, who were in the earth moving construction business."

Present day Mudjaw Bowmen clubhouse. Courtesy of the Mudjaw Bowmen and John Sinkovic.

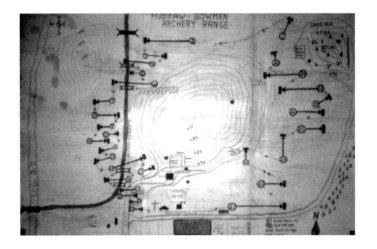

Plans for the archery range. Courtesy of the Mudjaw Bowmen and John Sinkovic.

MUDJAW BOWMEN
*Cordially invites you and your family
to attend its 32nd Annual*

BIG GAME AWARDS DINNER
hosted by John Sinkovic

*March 25, 1995
at 6:00 pm*

*Please provide a main dish to pass around.
Beer and Pop provided.
B.Y.O.B.
Casual Dress.*

*For additional information call:
Steve Oliver Pres: 255-8053
John Sinkovic: 691-7232*

*Admission - $1.00
Children admitted free*

**Awards Dinner invitation for 1995.
Courtesy of the Mudjaw Bowmen and
John Sinkovic.**

**Nada VanderHorst at Bay View
Park's practice range. Nada's the only
one who got a shot at a deer at the
Cranberry Ranch in 1957. Courtesy of
Nada VanderHorst.**

**Lynn VanderHorst's game record
with the Mudjaw Bowmen. Courtesy
of Nada VanderHorst.**

From l – r: John Jakeway, Jerry Ross, and Lynn VanderHorst at Bay View Park's practice range. Courtesy of Nada VanderHorst.

Mudjaw Bowmen burning their clubhouse and property's mortgage. Circa 1969. Courtesy of Nada VanderHorst.

Finally, in the words of Howie Lang ….

"Last of all, lets not forget all the members who have used their own trucks, autos, tools, lawn mowers, and time who have made this club a success.
Help comes in strange ways
You guys are doing a Great Job."

Aerial Views of Point Place

Naval Armory and Bay View Park in the forefront, Detwiler Golf Course on the left and Point Place on the background right circa 1950. Courtesy of the Toledo Lucas County Public Library.

Naval Armory and Oregon's coal loading docks circa 1950. Courtesy of the Toledo Lucas County Public Library.

The Point Place peninsula looking towards downtown Toledo. The Maumee River is on the left and the Ottawa River is on the right, circa 1937. Courtesy of the Toledo Lucas County Public Library.

Looking east from the Shoreland area across the Ottawa River. Gibb's Hardware is in the middle of the photo. Circa 1950. Courtesy of the Toledo Lucas County Public Library.

The Point Place Peninsula looking north to south. Circa 1937. The dock or inlet that is in the right side center of the photograph is for the carp ponds that were located in Morin Point. Courtesy of the Toledo Lucas County Public Library.

Point Place
Cardinal
Baseball Team

The 1935 Point Place *Cardinals* Baseball Team. The photo was taken in the open field behind the group of stores between 119th and 117th Streets. The ball field is currently where the Point Place Library is located. The house in the extreme upper left belonged to the Kolling Family.

First row from left to right: Bud Kramer, Ed Kerchevall, Chuck Rhodes, and Chuck Kerchevall. Second Row: Buss Pease, Chuck Swinghammer, Jim Rhodes, and Bud Dieball. Third Row: George Medon, Kennie Kerchevall, George Bender, and Fred Drogmiller.

Courtesy of Bill Williamson

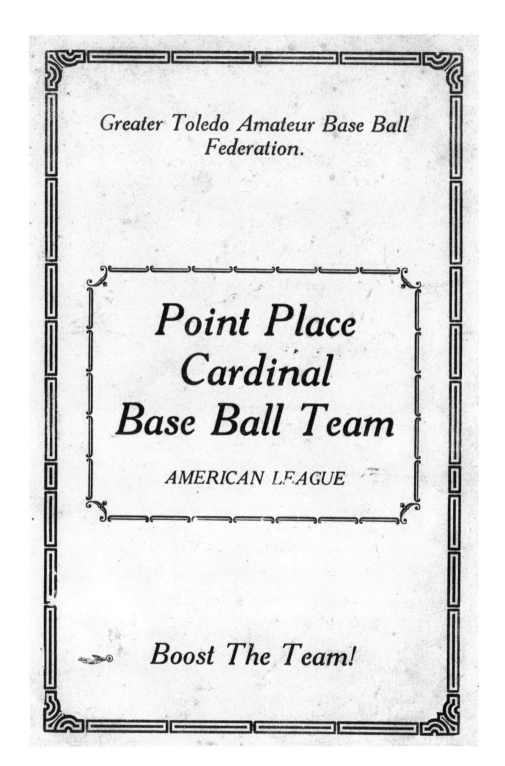

Greater Toledo Amateur Base Ball
Federation.

Point Place
Cardinal
Base Ball Team

AMERICAN LEAGUE

Boost The Team!

Courtesy of Bill Williamson.

SUMMIT STREET

Hi Hat Restaurant

Bill Merryman and the Hi-Hat Restaurant located at 5241 Summit Street. Courtesy of Carol [Merryman] Linkey.

Bill Merryman on the right behind the counter serving the lunch customers during the 50's. Courtesy of Carol [Merryman] Linkey.

In 1960 the Hi-Hat was torn down to make way for Merryman's King's Taste.
Located at the same location the new fast-food restaurant can be seen on the
extreme left of the photo. Courtesy of Carol [Merryman] Linkey.

Bill and Grace Merryman inside their new restaurant the King's taste. Circa 1960.
Courtesy of Carol [Merryman] Linkey.

A & P Grocery Store

Dr. Barney Hein's residence at 4828 Summit Street. When the A&P Grocery Store bought the property the house was moved to 114th Street. Courtesy of Howard Pinkley

A & P Grocery Store located at 4828 Summit Street. Until 2007 it was the home of Rite-Aid. Circa 1950. Courtesy of the Toledo Lucas County Public Library.

Shoreway Theater

Shoreway Theater 5228 Summit Street. Circa 1950. Courtesy of the Toledo Lucas County Public Library.

Karen Cobourne Hady

The following account of the Shoreway Theater is from an e-mail sent to Red Oberdier, past president of the Point Place Heritage Society, from Karen Cobourne Hady. Courtesy of the Point Place Heritage Society.

"Mr. Young owned the Shoreway before my Dad bought it. I vaguely remember him. But even then I would go to the Sunday Matinee. I was 10 when Dad bought the Shoreway. So that was about 1948. He kept his day job as projectionist at the Loop Theater and summers he did nights at the drive-ins. It was really a family business. My sister, Marianna was already out of school so she wasn't about much. Mom made all the signs and also sold signs for Cypher's Drive-In and the A&P.

When Mom and Dad had the Shoreway Theater due to union rules Dad couldn't be the projectionist in his own theater. So they hired Buckley. He was crippled from a childhood bout with polio so he had difficulties in moving around the booth. He always had to lean on one projector to move around. Every time he switched from one projector to the next [reel changes required a switch in projectors to keep the picture continuous] Dad would have to buzz him to readjust the picture because Buckley would throw the picture out of focus. Jesse Yoder, George Hogan, my brothers, Gordon [GG] and Duncan worked as ushers, bringing up candy stock from the basement, making popcorn, selling candy and drinks. My grandmother Maud Duncan also worked there. We all called her mud. Jesse and George and later others called Mom and Dad, Ma and Pa Cobourne. I remember when the guys gave lighters to Mom and Dad. Dad's said Pa Cobourne and the one for Mom said Ma Cobourne. I think either Gordon or Marianna got Dad's lighter. I gave Mom's lighter to my daughter. Bob Sommersett also worked there and I'm sure many more.

Some of my favorite childhood memories are when we got the theater. On summer nights sometimes Dad would offer to take us swimming at the Clearwater Quarry after we cleaned the theater. There would be Jesse, George, Gordon, Duncan, and myself. He had an arrangement with the owner of the quarry and we would be the only ones there. It was at that quarry that I learned to swim. I love remembering those times they were happy times.

The only other gathering place for kids was Teen Town. After Teen Town a lot of us would head for the Shoreway. It was my second home. At first it was so different for me because I was used to having Mom at home all the time. She spent long hours cleaning the Shoreway or being home painting signs. It was good for me though as I met so many people. I still laugh at the time a film salesman called. When I answered the phone he thought I was Mom and said, "darling how are you?" the film salesman called everybody darling. The real laugh was when I got all huffy at him and it turned out to be not a film salesman but my uncle.

I remember you could smoke in the theater if you stayed behind the partition from the seats. I remember the ushers going around and they would shine a light on anyone acting up. Which also meant if I was sitting with a boyfriend we would have to post a lookout if we wanted to kiss. I remember us having fun in the smoking area. I remember scrapping gum off of the seats. Duncan put in the ductwork for the air conditioning. Do you remember the smell of the popcorn popping? Dad always insisted on using coconut oil because he thought that it gave it a better taste. I remember the guys having to salt the entrance way when it snowed because it was so slippery when it snowed and they had to keep mopping the floor going from the doors inside through the lobby. Do you remember having to sweep up all the June bugs from the sidewalk?

When Dad went bankrupt he stored all the really neat posters like Rita Hayworth on the hay pile in the basement. Then there was a flood that took all the posters as well as most of Mom's artwork. I also remember when Dad told me he had finally paid off all the bills. He only used bankruptcy to delay until he could pay all of the bills even though he didn't have to. … Thanks for a chance to relive the time.

Shoreway Theater ad from November of 196?. Courtesy of the Point Place Herald and the Point Place Heritage Society.

Duffy Realty Company 5145 Summit Street at the corner of 122nd Street. Circa 1931. Courtesy of Gene and Marcia King.

Dr. Williamson M.D., Dr. Buck M.D., Dr. Mathews dentist, and Bambino's Pizza have all claimed 5145 as home. Courtesy of the Toledo Lucas County Public Library.

BAUERFELD'S
PAINTS — WALL PAPER
Westinghouse Appliances

FISHING and HUNTING LICENSES — SPORTING GOODS

4907 Summit Street   **POntiac 1861**

Bauerfelds 4907 Summit Street. Circa 1950. Courtesy of the Toledo Lucas County Public Library.

Bauerfeld's Appliance Store circa 1946. Courtesy of the Toledo Lucas County Public Library.

R. W. HARRISON
BOAT WORKS

3840 Summit Street
at Bay View Park

STORAGE and REPAIRING
Marine Paints and Supplies
New Engines

───── BOATS FOR SALE ─────

Harrison Boat Works 3840 Summit Street. Circa 1950. Courtesy of the Toledo Lucas County Public Library.

Harrison's Boat Works 3840 Summit Street circa 1912. Courtesy of the Toledo Lucas County Public Library.

Phone PO. 0258

IRISH TAVERN

JIM McCAFFREY, Prop.

⚓

Beer — Liquors — Wines

⚓

**4133 SUMMIT STREET
TOLEDO, OHIO**

Irish Tavern 4133 Summit Street. Circa 1950. Courtesy of the Toledo Lucas County Public Library.

The Irish Tavern was located across Summit Street from the entrance to the Casino Grounds. Circa 1950. Courtesy of the Toledo Lucas County Public Library.

LIGHTHOUSE INN

5013-5015 Summit Street

Point Place, Toledo, Ohio

BEER - LIQUOR - WINES

Phone: PO. 0170

Chinese and American Food

Chilly—Bing—Yee

Lighthouse Inn 5013 Summit Street. Circa 1950. Courtesy of the Toledo Lucas County Public Library.

CHAMPION and NEPTUNE MOTORS
FISHING TACKLE and LIVE BAITS
OUTBOARD MOTOR REPAIRING

DANNY MITCHELL

5432 Summit Street
PO. 6025

Mitchell Outboards 5432 Summit
Street. Circa 1950. Courtesy of the
Toledo Lucas County Public Library.

Pepper's Garage was located at 4849
or 4851 Summit Street and other than
repairing automobiles they were the
Willys Dealer in 1934. Circa 1934.
Courtesy of the Toledo Lucas County
Public Library.

Mitchell's Outboards. Circa 1950. Courtesy of the Toledo Lucas County Public
Library.

Abele Funeral & the New Barge Inn Bowling Lanes

A B E L E
FUNERAL HOMES

Invalid Service De Luxe
Finest Equipment
Still Most Reasonable Prices

Licensed
Lady Embalmer

DAY or NIGHT

ADams   POntiac
5161   0921

1910-1912 CHERRY — 4861 SUMMIT

Visit The Enlarged

NEW BARGE INN

4861 Summit Street

UNEXCELLED FOODS
LIQUOR — WINE — BEER

*MUSIC AND
DANCING*

Friday and Saturday
Dance Room Available For
Private Parties Except
Fridays and Saturdays

Abele's Funeral Home Circa 1935 and the New Barge Inn Circa 1950, both were located at 4861 Summit Street. Courtesy of the Toledo Lucas County Public Library.

In 1931 4861 Summit Street was the Abele Funeral Home, and in 1946 it became the Barge Inn Restaurant and Bowling Alley owned by Lou Colbey. Circa 1950. Courtesy of the Toledo Lucas County Public Library.

Nick Dakis & the Golden Door.
Courtesy of the Toledo BLADE.

Dockery's Satan & the Angels.
Courtesy of the Toledo BLADE.

Golden Door

Jeff Burch:

I played keyboards in Chuck Dockery's rock and roll band at the Golden Door in Point Place in the Spring of 1962. The Toledo Area was a hot bed of rock and roll in the early 60's. The national success of Johnny and the Hurricanes from Rossford, Johnny Gibson from Toledo, and the BG Ramblers added to the reputation of the area for good music. The fact that persons 18-21 years of age could drink 3.2 beer in Ohio and had to be 21+ in Michigan didn't hurt the weekend crowds either.

In the Summer of 1962, the owners of the Golden Door wanted to capitalize on the success of the Bamboo Club on Lagrange Street, and had heard that Chuck Dockery was back in Toledo. The Dockery band had just returned to town after a successful road trip that included the famous Roundtable in New York City and the Cloister in Chicago. By the Fall of 1961, George Morris, at the site of the former Pioneer Club opened the Peppermint Club in downtown Toledo, and persuaded the Dockery Band [Chuck Dockery, bass guitar and vocals; Preston Jones, lead guitar; Tommy Jordan, sax; Larry Samples, drums; and Jeff Burch, keyboards] to be the band at the new club. The Peppermint had a capacity more than double that of the Bamboo Club. The huge fun loving, dancing crowds followed the Dockery Band to the Peppermint Club, and we played seven nights a week. When Chuck decided to move to the Golden Door in the Spring of 1962 our fans followed. As the word traveled throughout southern Michigan that we were playing at the Golden Door the place was packed every night.

In mid-1962 to the detriment of local musicians, but not necessarily to the male patrons of the local bar scene, many bar owners switched to a live go-go girls with a recorded music format. There continued to be places to find live music in the area but not nearly as many places as the heyday period of 1960-1962.

Satan and the Angels [the Chuck Dockery Band] at New York's *Roundtable* in 1961. From l-r: Chuck Dockery, Don Stabile [replaced Larry Samples], Tommy Jordon [Jagielski], Preston Jones, with Jeff Burch reclining on the Grand Piano. Courtesy of Jeff Burch.

Eileen Durand:

One night my friend Sue and I were at the Barge Inn watching her husband and some other friends bowl. After a while Sue suggested going down to the "Golden Door" to listen to the band and the music.

While we were listening to the band, Sue recognized a young man standing at the bar. She called him over and I immediately recognized him as someone I had an enormous crush on in the eighth grade. After talking for awhile he asked me to dance. He told me he was about to be discharged from the Navy in about a week, and could he call me. I said "yes" and he did call. I felt like I was falling for him again. We went out and continued to date from then on. Ten months later we were married. We have been married 43 years.

Frank Weiss

Frank Weiss was the son of Michael Weiss one of Toledo's first settlers, and was the first child born in Michaelsburg. Named after his father, Michaelsburg was located in an area of Toledo north of Bancroft and Cherry Streets. In 1905 Frank Weiss moved with his family to Point Place and started the Weiss Fruit Farm. The Weiss farm was roughly bounded by Summit Street, 290th Street, 108th and 109th Streets. To supplement the family's income from the farm, Frank worked for the postal service for 40 years. In recognition of Frank's long service with the mail the BLADE in 1925 wrote an article describing his service and the estimated 2,400,000 pieces of mail that passed through his hands.

The photo on the left is Frank Weiss at 21 in 1885 when he started with the Postal Service. The picture on the right was taken in 1925 after more than forty years of service as a mail carrier. Courtesy of Eileen Durand.

This house was located on the left of the shingled house in the above photo at 4721 Summit Street and belonged to Frank Weiss. It was built from the same plans of his parent's house at 830 Frederick Street. Both of the houses featured on this page are now the greater part of Messiah Lutheran Church's parking lot. Courtesy of Eileen Durand.

This shingled house was the first house south at 4721 Summit Street from Weiss's Sohio Station and belonged to Henry Weiss. Courtesy of Eileen Durand.

Mary and Louis Braatz shown milking the cow were Eileen Durand's great grandparents. The large house on the left belonged to Elmer & Laura Braatz and was located at Summit Street and 107th Street, or the Big Odd Lots Store [Foodtown Grocery] and the farm field shown is Big Odd Lots current parking lot. The house barely seen above Mary's head would be at Summit and 108th Street. Summit Street runs left to right between the houses. The dirt lane to the right of the picture will become 109th Street. Courtesy of Eileen Durand.

Weiss Service Station Summit Street and 109th Street. Circa 1950. Courtesy of the Toledo Lucas County Public Library.

Weiss's Sohio Station at 4731 Summit Street. Circa 1956. Courtesy of the Toledo Lucas County Public Library.

The old Messiah Lutheran Church at 4703 Summit Street at 108th Street. The new church was built on the corner and old church [above] was directly north and was still there until 1962, then the old church was torn down for additional parking. Courtesy of the Toledo Lucas County Public Library.

Pepper's Garage was remodeled and became the J&S Drug Store. Circa 1949. J & S Drug Store later became the home of Dr. Joseph Hampton and his Bayside Dental practice. Courtesy of the Toledo Lucas County Public Library.

Gene's Hardware & Edgewater Furniture

The Edgewater Market Supply Boat. On the right Bus Durfey and Steve Werkman are taking a load of groceries to the C&O Dock. Circa 1934. Courtesy of Kathy [Werkman] Sienkowski.

Edgewater Appliance and Furniture Store and Gene's Hardware. Located at 5212 Summit Street the McDonald's restaurant now occupies the property. Courtesy of the Toledo Lucas County Public Library.

Edgewater Appliance & Hardware in 1947 with Gene Werkman as manager. Located at 116th Street and Summit Street where RiteAid is now located. Courtesy of Kathy [Werkman] Sienkowski.

Gene's Hardware at 5212 Summit Street with Edgewater Furniture on the right in 1967. The sandalwood panels on the front of the building were vitrolite. The property is now a McDonalds. Courtesy of Kathy [Werkman] Sienkowski.

Edgewater Cleaners

One of Edgewater Cleaner's first delivery trucks parked in what is now McDonalds Restaurant's parking lot. The house on the extreme left was behind the cleaners and was the Gale Family home. Circa 1938. Courtesy of Kathy Bradley.

Edgewater Cleaners. Circa 1948. Notice the brick paving on Summit Street and what appears to be a barber shop on the right. If you look closely Margaret Gale is holding her younger sister Kathy. Courtesy of Kathy Bradley.

Harry Gale inside Edgewater Cleaners at 5216 Summit Street. Circa 1954. Courtesy of his daughter Kathy Bradley.

Harry Gale and his Shriner's Unit parading in front of St. John's Catholic Church, looking south down Summit Street. Circa 1959. Courtesy of his daughter Kathy Bradley.

Cypher's

Lee and Peggy Cypher opened their drive-in in 1948 as a Richardson's Root Beer outlet. With no interior seating they quickly remodeled and enlarged the drive-in to include counter seating. Courtesy of Margaret [Peggy] Cypher.

Five hot dogs for a dollar, remodeled with interior seating, and with the house moved to 302nd Street, Cypher's was ready for business. Circa 1950. Courtesy of Margaret [Peggy] Cypher.

After extensive demolition of the old Cypher's, the new Cypher's Restaurant was once again serving customers in 1969. The waitress on the right was Carol Knox. Courtesy of Margaret [Peggy] Cypher.

Lee Cypher. Courtesy of Margaret [Peggy] Cypher.

EARL'S MARKET

GROCERIES — MEATS
FRUITS — VEGETABLES

5039 Summit Street

PO. 2611-2612

Earl's Market was located at 5039 Summit Street. Circa 1950. Courtesy of the Toledo Lucas County Public Library.

With Hurl Ralston behind the meat counter and his wife, Nancy, at the cash register they both ran Earl's Meat Market at 5039 Summit Street at 119th Street. Courtesy of the Toledo Lucas County Public Library.

ELLIS BARBER SHOP

Two Barbers—No Waiting

4910 Summit Street

Ellis's Barber Shop. Circa 1950. Courtesy of the Toledo Lucas County Public Library.

Before the library took over both sides of the Kleis Building, Cecil Ellis had his barber shop there. Circa 1958. Courtesy of the Toledo Lucas County Public Library.

St. John's Catholic Church

St. John's Catholic Church at the corner of 124th Street and Summit Street. Circa 1940. Courtesy of the Point Place Heritage Society.

St. John's Elementary School was located in the church's parking lot. Courtesy of the Toledo Lucas County Public Library.

St. John's Catholic Church at the corner of 124th Street and Summit Street. Circa 1940. Courtesy of the Point Place Heritage Society.

Edgewater Drive Businesses

Compliments of

Kingston Barber Shop

5508 Edgewater Drive

Kingston's Barber Shop 5508 Edgewater Drive. Courtesy of the Toledo Lucas County Public Library.

Kingston's Barber Shop about 1957. Courtesy of the Toledo Lucas County Public Library.

Daniel's Pharmacy

5532 Edgewater Dr.

PRESCRIPTIONS

DEPENDABLE SERVICE

AT ALL TIMES

Ad from the Ottawa River Yacht Club's 1947 Regatta Brochure. Courtesy of the Toledo Lucas County Public Library.

Daniel's Pharmacy 5532 Edgewater Drive about 1957. Courtesy of the Toledo Lucas County Public Library.

From the Point Place Memories by Marcia King. *This side of Gergen's Grocery Store up across from the schoolhouse was John Daniel's. if you had a stomach ache or something was wrong with you, you didn't need go to a doctor, old John would give you something to fix you up. Clarence and Stella Eikost.*

Vander Horst Greenhouse, 5525 Edgewater Drive. Courtesy of the Ottawa River Yacht Club's Regatta booklet from 1947.

Vander Horst's or Edington's Greenhouse 5525 Edgewater Drive. Courtesy of the Toledo Lucas County Library.

BAYSIDE MARKET

5552 Edgewater Dr.

Paul Richards, Prop.

PO. 3856

Bayside Market, 5552 Edgewater Drive. Courtesy of the Ottawa River Yacht Club's Regatta booklet from 1947.

Ross's Confectionery 5620 Edgewater Drive about 1954. Courtesy of the Toledo Lucas County Public Library.

J. O. MACHINE CO.

Experimental

General Machine Work

Jigs — Fixtures — Dies

5644 Edgewater Dr.   PO. 1620

J & O Machine Shop, 5644 Edgewater Drive. Courtesy of the Ottawa River Yacht Club's Regatta booklet from 1947.

J & O Machine Shop 5644 Edgewater Drive about 1958. Courtesy of the Toledo Lucas County Public Library.

Ruff's Boat Dock later to become Bush's Boat Dock 5809 Edgewater Drive about 1958. Courtesy of the Toledo Lucas County Public Library.

Water Front Drive In Restaurant 5802 Edgewater Drive, June 1962. Courtesy of Carol Griffin.

Jake Erd's

Ottawa River Fish Market

FRESH and SMOKED FISH DAILY

LIVE BAITS

George (Jake) Erd

5911 Edgewater Dr.

PO. 7271

Imitation Gold and Silver Letters

For Boats, Autos and Trucks

Jake's Sign Service

(Signs of All Kinds)

5911½ Edgewater Drive

PO. 7271

Ottawa River Fish Market, Jake Erd, 5911 Edgewater Drive. Courtesy of the Ottawa River Yacht Club's Regatta booklet from 1947.

Jake Erd's sign shop, 5911 ½ Edgewater Drive. Courtesy of the Ottawa River Yacht Club's Regatta booklet from 1947.

George "Jake" Erd was one of the Point's most beloved characters. Even though he had his own dock system at 5911 Edgewater Drive, about where the Turtle Club was berthed, Jake Erd was often seen at many of the other yacht clubs in the area helping out when he could. The photo was taken in 1961 inside his office/home which was built on piers adjacent to his dock. Courtesy of Mrs. Lee Brann.

Jake Erd's dock during a time of low water on the Ottawa River in 1941. If you follow the shoreline on the extreme left of the photo you can just see the stone work for the Summit Street extension bridge. Courtesy of Lois Rolsten and the Point Place Heritage Society.

Jake Erd and Ralph Brann on Gard Island in 1961. Notice the wide expanse of sandy beach. After the spring storms the Ottawa River islands were great places to explore for arrowheads and other Indian artifacts. Courtesy of Mrs. Lee Brann.

Jake Erd's Dock was opened by his father, George, on Memorial Day 1910. May 30th was called Decoration Day. The docks were called Erd's Boat House and when Jake closed up his dock and bait shop it was the oldest boat and bait dealer in Northwestern Ohio.

From the Point Place Memories by Marcia King. *...and then George Erd's saloon where the Turtle Club is now situated? They called that the Driftwood Inn. It was driftwood. Old George, he would go over to Turtle Light when they tore down the old lighthouse on Turtle Island and get most of the wood over there and they called his saloon the Driftwood Inn. Clarence and Stella Eikost.*

Ralph Brann pumping gas at Jake Erd's gasoline dock on the Ottawa River in 1961. Courtesy of Mrs. Lee Brann.

George "Jake" Erd and his assistant manager Anna Marie "PeeWee" Kuebbeler inside the dock's office. Courtesy of Mrs. Lee Brann.

Bob Fischer's Outboard Repair and marine supplies 5817 Edgewater Drive about 1956. Courtesy of the Toledo Lucas County Public Library.

Alice and Ray's

WATER FRONT BAR

The Bar Over the Water

5827 Edgewater Drive

We Specialize in
— FINE FOODS —
Anything can happen here
and usually does

BEER — WINE

PO. 0223

Alice & Ray's waterfront restaurant and café, located at 5827 Edgewater Drive the current site of Chet's Marine Service. Courtesy of the Ottawa River Yacht Club's Regatta booklet from 1947.

Chet's Marine Service

Chet and Betty Sabin, long time Point Place residents, purchased the property that once housed Alice & Ray's in January of 1950. Chet was the recipient of the *"Old Man of the River"* Award in 1979 and Betty received the recognition in 1999.

Chet Sabin and his gaff rigged iceboat, and his 15 Meter *Fast Action* off King's on the Maumee Bay in 1935. Courtesy of Betty Sabin.

Utility racing on the Ottawa River. Courtesy of Betty Sabin.

On the left is the first building erected on Chet's waterfront property in 1950. Don Hoilman is shown coming out the door. On the right is Chet Sabin working on the docks. About the same date. Courtesy of Betty Sabin.

Chet's Marine Service added the Texaco fuel capability to the dock in 1951. An unidentified plane using the facility. Courtesy of Betty Sabin.

Charles Marleau and Charlie Desmond at Claude Lytle's Texaco Service Station circa 1931. Courtesy of the Point Place Heritage Society.

Carol and Richard Marleau on the Ottawa River with Lytle's dock on the right. Courtesy of Richard Marleau.

Al's Marina featuring Sinclair Gasoline at 5860 Edgewater Drive circa 1958. Courtesy of the Toledo Lucas County Public Library.

The River Inn Restaurant at 5930 Edgewater Drive across from Keene's circa 1948. Courtesy of Richard Marleau.

COLD
BEER

PHONE PONT. 0122

KEENE'S CAFE

FISH, CHICKEN, STEAK DINNERS
SANDWICHES OF ALL KINDS

WM. KEENE, PROP.

COR. EDGEWATER & 315TH ST.
POINT PLACE

Business card for Keene's Café. Located at 315th Street at Edgewater, currently the site of the Captain's Carryout. Courtesy of Richard Marleau.

Jake Erd in his column "Along the Waterfront" mentioned in 1951 that Vicki "Ma" Kahle is the cook in Keene's Café and *"but, she sure knows how to cook."* Leaving the New Barge Inn, Gert Briggs, is assisting Ma Kahle in Keene's kitchen.

Keene's Café with Bill Keene at the bar. Courtesy of the Point Place Heritage Society.

Gibb's Hardware, 5902-5908 Edgewater Drive. Courtesy of the Ottawa River Yacht Club's Regatta booklet from 1947.

Singleton's or Gibb's Hardware 5902 Edgewater Drive. Courtesy of the Toledo Lucas County Public Library.

5906 Edgewater Drive circa 1958. Courtesy of the Toledo Lucas County Public Library.

Edgewater Canvas Shop 5911 Edgewater Drive about 1955. Courtesy of the Toledo Lucas County Public Library.

Neumeyer's Confectionery 5912 Edgewater Drive about 1915. Courtesy of the Point Place Heritage Society.

Neumeyer's Grocery Store circa 1934. Courtesy of the Toledo BLADE.

Valleywood Market 5912 Edgewater Drive. Courtesy of the Toledo Lucas County Public Library.

Walt Duling boat Builder 5929 Edgewater Drive about 1954. Courtesy of the Toledo Lucas County Public Library.

Walt Duling's residence and boat dock, 5931 Edgewater Drive about 1954. Courtesy of the Toledo Lucas County Public Library.

This was the Johnson's Restaurant in the early 1900's. In 1954 it was the residence of Frank Leach, 5946 Edgewater Drive. Courtesy of the Toledo Lucas County Public Library.

The Toledo Outboard Club in 1954, 5981 Edgewater Drive, it has since been extensively enlarged and remodeled and is now River View Yacht Club. Courtesy of the Toledo Lucas County Public Library.

Paul's Pure Oil Service, 5986 Edgewater Drive about 1963. Courtesy of the Toledo Lucas County Public Library.

`Elizabeth Dayan's Boat Livery and Dock at 6051 Edgewater Drive, circa 1941. Courtesy of the Point Place Heritage Society.

Louie's Boat Dock at 6051 Edgewater Drive about 1954. Courtesy of the Toledo Lucas County Public Library.

Louie's Boat Dock about 1954. Gave the weather forecast on the chalkboard and always flew the appropriate weather signal flag. Courtesy of the Toledo Lucas County Public Library.

Henry Sheridan, 6202 Edgewater Drive, about 1931. Courtesy of the Toledo Lucas County Public Library.

Mominee's Boat Livery Circa 1930. Courtesy of William "Bill" Jockett.

BILL'S BOAT LIVERY

Edgewater Drive

At End of Bus Line

BAIT, MINNOWS, TACKLE

Bill Jocket & Son, Props.

Bill Jockett's Dock and Boat Livery. Courtesy of the Ottawa River Yacht Club's Regatta booklet from 1947.

Bill Jockett 1937. Courtesy of William "Bill" Jockett.

Across the road [Edgewater Drive] was a nice grove under which were benches where you could have your picnic and from there all along the waterfront to Webber's Tavern were cottages. There was a boat house operated by Bill and Jack Wersall and one operated by Charlie Belson. This was in front of [John, Mrs Eikost's dad] Mominee's Saloon. This was taken over by Harry Mominee who had 85 rowboats and they were, believe it or not, all rented by daylight. He had two towboats. The WHITECAP operated by me and the BERNICE operated by Leonard Motter towed them as far as Bay Point. **Clarence and Stella Eikost, Point Place Memories, Marcia King, PPHS.**

Mominee's Boat Livery at 6209 Edgewater Drive later to become the home of Jockett's Marina. Photo is from about 1930. Courtesy of Nancy Schill.

Lucille and Ray Nation at the foot of Jockett's Dock in 1935. Courtesy of William "Bill" Jockett.

Jockett's fishing boat rental. Circa 1944. Courtesy of William "Bill" Jockett

Jockett towing the fishing boats to Bay Point. Courtesy of William "Bill' Jockett.

Ice Cream   Cigars and Tobacco

DALY'S MARKET

Meats, Groceries, Produce
Gasoline and Oils

6224 Edgewater Drive
Phone PO. 0261

"Mike" Daly, "Prop."

Daly's Market 6224 Edgewater Drive. George Ellis ran a grocery store at the same address in the 1930's. Courtesy of the Ottawa River Yacht Club's Regatta booklet from 1947.

6241 Edgewater Drive was in 1954 the residence of John Berner. Courtesy of the Toledo Lucas County Public Library.

6301 Edgewater Drive was the clubhouse of the Dynamiter Club in 1946. Courtesy of Nancy Schill.

WEBBER'S
GLASSLESS TAVERN

GOOD FOODS

Beer and Ale by Case or Bottle

Open Summer and Winter

6341 Edgewater Dr.

And of course 6341 Edgewater Drive was the home of Webber's glass-less tavern. Courtesy of the Ottawa River Yacht Club's Regatta booklet from 1947.

Webber's Glassless Tavern at 6341 Edgewater Drive just over the Ohio Michigan State Line. Circa 1948. Starting with a small house and a fishing shack John Webber opened his restaurant or tavern in 1933, and it wasn't long before the orchards that were located east of the tavern became his part-time occupation. Courtesy of Larry and Becky Merryman.

Looking north with Edgewater Drive continuing into Michigan's Lost Peninsula Webber's continued to do a great business selling perch and walleye, beer, and those world famous onion rings. More and more customers would find themselves lined up outside waiting to enjoy the excellent food. Circa 1948. Courtesy of Larry and Becky Merryman.

John Webber behind the bar on a busy day. Circa 1950. Courtesy of Larry and Becky Merryman.

This picture is of the Tornado that swept through Erie, Michigan in 1953 and is very similar to the tornado that swept through Shoreland and the Lost Peninsula on Palm Sunday of 1965. Webber's location would be on the right just past the trees. Courtesy of Al Antoine and RVYC.

Some of the destruction visited on Webber's from the Palm Sunday tornado of 1965. Courtesy of Larry and Becky Merryman.

The 1965 tornado's destruction from the air. Courtesy of Larry and Becky Merryman.

The high water and floods of 1949, 1972, 1973, and the destruction resulting from the Palm Sunday Tornado did not stop John Webber from rebuilding. Larry and Becky Merryman purchased Webbers in 1980 and after extensive remodeling, together they have enhanced the fine reputation that generations of Webber's patrons have grown to expect. Courtesy of Larry and Becky Merryman.

Gasoline Service Stations in Point Place

Bob Meier's Gulf Gas Station. NE corner of Suder and Ottawa River. Courtesy of the Point Place Heritage Society.

Logan's Market at the corner of Suder and Shoreland. Courtesy of the Point Place Heritage Society.

Formerly a Sohio Service Station at the NE corner of Shoreland and Summit. This photo was taken by George Green after the Palm Sunday Tornado. Courtesy of the Point Place Heritage Society.

106th Street and Summit. Courtesy of the Toledo Lucas County Public Library.

Advertisement for Weiss's Sohio. Courtesy of Louise Brubaker and the Point Place Heritage Society.

Weiss's Sohio Station at the corner of 109th Street and Summit. Courtesy of the Toledo Lucas County Public Library.

Al's [Lytle] Sinclair gas or marine service. Located at the corner of 140th Street and Edgewater. Courtesy of the Toledo Lucas County Public Library.

Al's [Lytle] as a Texaco Station. Courtesy of the Point Place Heritage Society.

**Paul's Pure Service Station at the corner of 145th Street and Edgewater Drive.
Courtesy of the Toledo Lucas County Public Library.**

**Bart's Marathon or the Canal Carryout. Located at 308th Street and 131st Street.
Courtesy of the Toledo Lucas County Public Library.**

Krick's Marine Service. Edgewater Drive north of 149th Street. Courtesy of the Toledo Lucas County Public Library.

Denny Dieball and Jim Davis bringing the APPLEKNOCKER out of Krick's garage on Edgewater Drive in 1975. From the author's collection.

The Phillip's 66 Station at 106th Street and Summit Street. Courtesy of the Toledo Lucas County Public Library.

Morrie's Cities Service Station. Located at 107th Street and Summit Street. Courtesy of the Toledo Lucas County Public Library.

**Gulf Station located at the corner of 114ᵗʰ Street and Summit Street. Courtesy of the
Toledo Lucas County Public Library.**

**Sunoco Station at the corner of 116ᵗʰ Street and Summit Street. Courtesy of the
Toledo Lucas County Public Library.**

The Hamrick Brother's Hi-Speed service station was located in the old A&P or Rite Aid parking lot on the east side of Summit Street at 113th Street.

Hamrick Brother's business card. Circa 1930. Courtesy of Richard Hamrick and Family.

John Hamrick at his Hi-Speed Gas Station at 113th Street and Summit. Courtesy of Richard Hamrick and Family.

John and Margaret Hamrick at their Hi-Speed Station. Courtesy of Richard Hamrick and Family.

Yeager's Texaco Service Station was located on the current Huntington Bank property at 121st Street and Summit Street. Courtesy of the Toledo Lucas County Public Library

Topping's Marathon Station was located in the northwest corner of 124th Street and Summit where the Sky Bank is now located. Courtesy of the Toledo Lucas County Public Library.

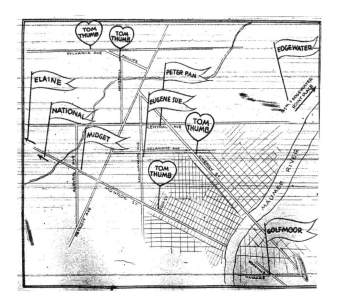

The Edgewater Miniature Golf Course was also located in the northwest corner of 124th Street and Summit Street. Courtesy of the Toledo News-Bee, Circa 1930.

In 1958 this property was the location of the Edgewater Speedway 79 Service Station. For those of you that can remember when gas stations competed for your business, Speedway 79 gave away water glasses with scenes of Michigan. From the author's collection.

The water glasses were the *Soo Locks, Mackinac Bridge, and Hartwick Pines.* We're still looking for the 4th glass. From the author's collection.

According to the 1946 City Directory 5432 Summit Street was the residence of Daniel Mitchell, soon to become the Pure Oil Station. Courtesy of the Toledo Lucas County Public Library.

Located at 5432 Summit Street at the corner of 131st Street was Ralph's Pure Oil Service. Courtesy of the Toledo Lucas County Public Library.

Originally a Standard Oil gas station on the southwest corner of Summit Street and 131st Street was the location of Jim's Sohio Service Station. The author pumped gasoline for 80 cents per hour in 1963 and worked 16-20 hours per week while attending Woodward High School. Courtesy of the Toledo Lucas County Public Library and Kip [Rudy] Proestos.

In 1972 Rudy's Hot Dog was also located at Summit Street and 131st Street. From l – r: Nancy Proestos, Kip's mother and Ruth. Courtesy of Kip [Rudy] Proestos.

Working at the Sohio Station wasn't all bad because across 131st Street was Rudy's Ice Cream Parlor. Courtesy of NorthPointe Used Cars and the Point Place Herald.

Cottages

The Jacob Folger Family Cottage. Circa 1900. Courtesy of Fred Folger III.

Jacob Folger Pork Packer Company. Circa 1890. Coutesy of the Toledo Lucas County Public Library.

Folger's Meat Packing Plant on Phillips Avenue immediately west of railroad tracks and Detroit Avenue. Circa 1912. Courtesy of the Toledo Lucas County Public Library.

With the Folger pork packing business expanded into all lines of meat products and well rooted in the Toledo business climate, Jacob Folger built for his family's enjoyment a cottage in Point Place. Located adjacent to the Ottawa River at Shoreland and the Toledo Beach interurban rail road line, the Folger cottage was built in the Victorian fashion of the day.

Folger Family boat house was located opposite the cottage on Shoreland Avenue. The stairway in the lower right would take you to the boat dock. Jacob Folger is third from the right. Courtesy of Fred Folger III.

The Folger Family yacht, ALERT. Courtesy of Fred Folger III.

The clubhouse, on the left, was built in about 1915, and was used for all the large social gatherings that would occur at the Folger cottage. Courtesy of Fred Folger III.

The present day location of the Folger Family cottage is the Shoreland Medical Center's parking lot. From the author's collection.

The naphtha launch CORRINE on the Ottawa River circa 1900. The white flowers are water lilies or lotus flowers Courtesy of Mark and Melinda Walczak.

The IDLE HOUR cottage in Point Place circa 1900. Courtesy of Mark and Melinda Walczak.

The Ladies Jolly Ten Club outing. Circa 1900. Courtesy of Mark and Melinda Walczak.

Casino ticket from the 1890's. Courtesy of Mark and Melinda Walczak.

The Riverside Pleasure Club, Circa 1890. Courtesy of Mark and Melinda Walczak.

Rowing on the Ottawa River. Circa 1900. Courtesy of Mark and Melinda Walczak.

KRIENER'S COTTAGE
the GROTTO
115th Street

Grotto Cottage and the Krieners. Circa 1918. Courtesy of Ella Kriener.

Walking down the incline from 115th Street to the beach along the Maumee Bay
1918. Courtesy of Ella Kriener.

Richard Kriener on the Maumee Bay beach in front of their cottage 1915. Courtesy of Ella Kriener.

Richard Kriener along side Mrs. Hanhouser's cottage 1918. Courtesy of Ella Kriener.

May and Ella Anderson off of Gard Island 1935. Courtesy of Ella [Anderson] Kriener.

Ella [Anderson] Kriener ice skating on the Maumee Bay 1937. Courtesy of Ella Kriener.

KAMP 4

The boys from Camp Four. The house looks like it was located on Lakeside near 145th Street on the Maumee Bay. Circa 1925 or so. Courtesy of Nancy Schill.

Camp Four from the Maumee Bay. Circa 1925. Courtesy of Nancy Schill.

Harry and Bill Schill iceboating on the Maumee Bay. Courtesy of Nancy Schill

Cutting ice on the Maumee Bay. According to various references the Crites Family's residence on Lakeside Drive was at one time a huge icehouse used to supply the needs of the Point. Courtesy of Nancy Schill.

Cutting and gathering the blocks of ice from the Maumee Bay. Courtesy of Nancy Schill.

Sailboat under construction along Edgewater Drive with the Ottawa River in the background. Unknown person or location. Courtesy of Nancy Schill.

Hill Top Stables
located in Detwiler Marsh
near Wausonoquette Drive and Bay View Court

Looking east on Bay View Court off 290th Street [Wausonoquette Drive] the location of the Hill Top Stable. From the author's collection.

Hilltop Stables was here. My brother-in-law, Gene Brand, lives in the house now. The guy who owned the stables was Dick Quinn. He died. Dick Quinn ran a garage under a shade tree. The horses were nags. The guy didn't have any money. Hilltop Stables was where the circle is on Torisdale. It was just a couple of old barns and an old house. It was around for 10-12 years. [Interview with PETE WETZLER by Marcia King, PPHS, 1989]

Torisdale Court was from 4529-290th Street east to the Maumee Bay, and Dick Quinn was listed on Torisdale Court.

Hill Top Stable. Circa 1946. Courtesy of Larry Pedee and the Point Place Heritage Society.

Hill Top Stable with rider Jerry Shonter. Courtesy of Larry Pedee and the Point Place Heritage Society.

Hill Top Stable with Kip, unknown rider. Circa 1939. Courtesy of Larry Pedee and the Point Place Heritage Society.

Business

The Dart Boat Building Company

Webb C. Hayes II, the grandson of President Rutherford B. Hayes and graduate of the United States Naval Academy, announced to the News-Bee in 1928 that the Indian Lake Company of Lima Ohio had been purchased and that they would begin building the popular mahogany Dart speedboats in Toledo. Hugh Bennett, president of Toledo Scale and Toledo Scale manufacturing, said that initially three boats a day would be built in the Summit Street plant along with the possibility of airplane fuselage construction.

Dart buildings off Haynes and Summit Streets looking towards the Maumee River in 1931. Courtesy of *The Real Runabouts II* by Robert Speltz and the Toledo Lucas County Public Library.

The Dart Boat Building Company started production in 1929 and within just a few months boot-legger's preferred the Dart speedboat above all others. Handling and flat-out speed were the requirements that the rum-runners needed to out run the Coast Guard and other law enforcement, and the Dart was the fastest boat on the Lakes.

The plant was located just off Summit Street and behind the old Vernor's bottling plant. Coincidently, manufacturing of the speedboat took place just across the street from the Kelsey & Freeman lumber company warehouse which at that time was used by the Licavoli Gang as a 10,000 gallon a day distillery.

Dart factory buildings off Haynes and Summit Streets in 2007. From the author's collection.

Advertisement showing the Dart beating the English Flying Scotsman Train. Courtesy of *The Real Runabouts II* by Robert Speltz and the Toledo Lucas County Public Library.

The Dart speedboat was shipped all over the world from its Summit Street home and company records show that a Dart was the first speedboat to be used on the Dead Sea.

A workman in 1931 hand sanding the forward deck of a Dart Speedboat. Courtesy of *The Real Runabouts II* by Robert Speltz and the Toledo Lucas County Public Library.

Two Coast Guard men, George Shaw and Dave St.Aubin, sanding the deck of a Dart Speedboat. Courtesy of the Point Place Heritage Society.

In July of 1929 Hugh Bennett, who was vice president of the Dart Boat Building Company, bought Rattlesnake Island. Bennett purchased the historic island from the Dollar Family of Port Clinton. The forested 40 acre rocky outcropping would be home to the Bennett Family during the hot Toledo summers.

Hugh Bennett's summer home on Rattlesnake Island 1931. Courtesy of Bob Terry, author of *"Honest Weight, the Story of Toledo Scale."*

The Dart factory was unique in its construction. Measuring 300 by 60 feet the solid concrete floor used specially constructed steel roof trusses and had no interior roof supports. Glass skylights lined the roof to provide interior lighting suitable for the fine work needed on the Dart Speedboats. As Prohibition was repealed and the Depression deepened, the Dart Boat Company ceased production in about 1937.

The 26' *"Silver Dart"* featured in the June 1931 issue of Motorboating magazine. Courtesy of the Toledo Lucas County Public Library.

Crabb Field
Point Place's 1ˢᵗ Airport

Located in the south west corner of the intersection of Alexis Road and Telegraph, Crabb Field was just minutes west of the *"Avenue of Booze"* or Detroit Avenue.

Walter Crabb and his DeHaviland DH-4 with a Liberty engine. Courtesy of Charles and Katherine Stahl.

Crabb Field & School of Instruction advertisement. Courtesy of Charles and Katherine Stahl.

Alexis Road runs left [east] to right [west] and Telegraph runs on the right side from the top [south] to the bottom [north]. Crabb School is located in the lower left of the intersection next to several bi-planes. Crabb Field is located in the top right of the intersection. Courtesy of Charles and Katherine Stahl.

Early Fly-In at Crabb Field. Courtesy of Charles and Katherine Stahl.

Crabb Field, August 2, 1926. The plane is a WACO-9. Weaver Aircraft Company. Courtesy of the Toledo Lucas County Public Library.

Unidentified man and Ford Tri-Motor at Crabb Field. Courtesy of Charles and Katherine Stahl.

November 24, 1926 the plane landed at Crabb Field taxied across Alexis Avenue to Crabb's gas station, filled the tank, and left the same way. Courtesy of Charles and Katherine Stahl.

With the passage of time Crabb Field eventually closed its doors and Walter Crabb replaced it with a new concept in amusements …. the Whippy-Dip. His concept was quite simple … you would drive your own car over the dips and around the curves.

The Whippy-Dip. Courtesy of Charles and Katherine Stahl.

A financial failure from its inception, Walter Crabb demolished the wooden structure of the Whippy-Dip and leased the field to an adjacent farmer. The farmer couldn't understand why he was getting flat tires all the time from the large nails that he was finding in the field.

A plane that Walter Crabb was rebuilding. Courtesy of Charles and Katherine Stahl.

Walter Crabb's gas station on Telegraph, north of Alexis Road. Courtesy of Charles and Katherine Stahl.

Walbridge Dairy Farm
Point Place's 2nd Airport

Bounded on the west by Stickney Avenue, Matzinger Road on the north, and the old Ann Arbor Rail Road yard on the east, the Walbridge Family farm was destined to become one of Toledo's first municipal airports and coveted manufacturing sites.

The first commercial use was that of the Walbridge Dairy Farm with its famous octagonal barns. From the *Plat Book of the City & Suburbs 1913*, Courtesy of the Toledo Lucas County Public Library.

Walbridge Dairy Farm, Main House, Water Tower, and several out buildings. From the *Plat Book of the City & Suburbs 1913*, Courtesy of the Toledo Lucas County Public Library.

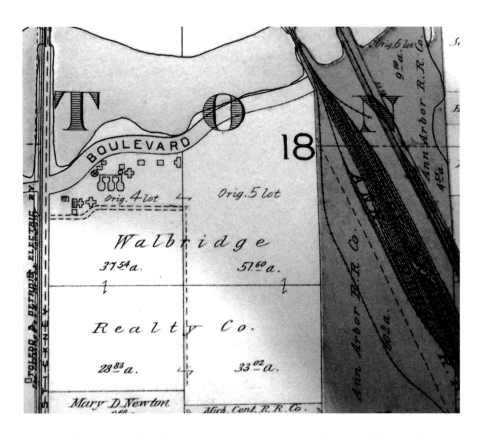

Walbridge Dairy Farm On Stickney Avenue at the Ottawa River. From the *Plat Book of the City & Suburbs 1913*, Courtesy of the Toledo Lucas County Public Library.

The three main octagonal barns on the Walbridge Dairy Farm. From the *Plat Book of the City & Suburbs 1913*, Courtesy of the Toledo Lucas County Public Library.

Water tower, foreman's home, and the octagonal barns of the Walbridge Dairy Farm. From the *Plat Book of the City & Suburbs 1913*, Courtesy of the Toledo Lucas County Public Library.

The Walbridge Dairy Farm continued in operation until the open salvos of World War One when it was converted into a training camp for Lieutenant Colonel Albrecht of Battery E of the 135th Ohio Field Artillery. Battery E was formed from the First Ohio Volunteer Cavalry. The dairy barns were converted into horse stables and the wide exspanse of land was perfect for calvary charges.

Stickney or Toledo Airport. Courtesy of the Toledo BLADE.

In the late twenties, the Walbridge Farm was converted into the Stickney Avenue Airport as Toledo entered the magical age of aviation. With the consent of City Council and the approval of the City Airport Commission fifteen thousand dollars was appropriated in 1927 to lease the Walbridge Farm and build the necessary buildings.

The Airport Commission stressing that Toledo's first landing field was only temporary, constructed two grass landing strips of 2,000 and 3,000 feet and built an airplane hangar that was 125 feet long. The hangar was completed with 65 foot steel doors at each end painted a brilliant yellow, and stenciled across the hangar's roof in huge white block letters was *Toledo Airport.*

With the Detroit Toledo Interurban rail road line running parallel to Stickney Avenue, some 40,000 Toledoans braved threatening weather to attend the airport's dedication ceremonies on October 29, 1927. Famed flying ace Eddie Rickenbacker and Toledo's own Roy Knabenshue changed their flight plans at the last minute due to the heavy fog and decided not to attend. Disappointed, the crowd roared its delight when the *"Pride of Detroit"* piloted by Will Brock and Fred Koehler landed. Having just completed a round the world flight, Will Brock was quoted as saying *".. while you have some hazards around the field, you have an advantage which few cities have – that is that your airport is close to the city to make it really practical for fast transportation."*

Leather helmets, goggles, silk scarves, and pants tucked into high top boots were the uniform of the day as the brave young men in their Curtis or Jenny biplanes would take passengers aloft for the unheard of fee of five dollars. Even with the air-shows that featured wing-walkers and parachute jumps the Stickney Avenue Airport was a huge financial failure.

Point Place residents Winston Smith, a flight instructor and teacher of flight mechanics at Macomber High School, and Toledo diemaker Carl Baldwin shared a J-2 Cub at the Stickney Airport. Reminiscing about the prohibition days of Stickney Airport Winston Smith recalled *"We were met at the runway by a big guy who ordered us to get out. In the argument that followed, one of the kids got knocked down. The man hauled out a gun, so we took off. Later we learned that a plane loaded with booze had been directly overhead. By showing up unexpectedly, we prevented the landing."*

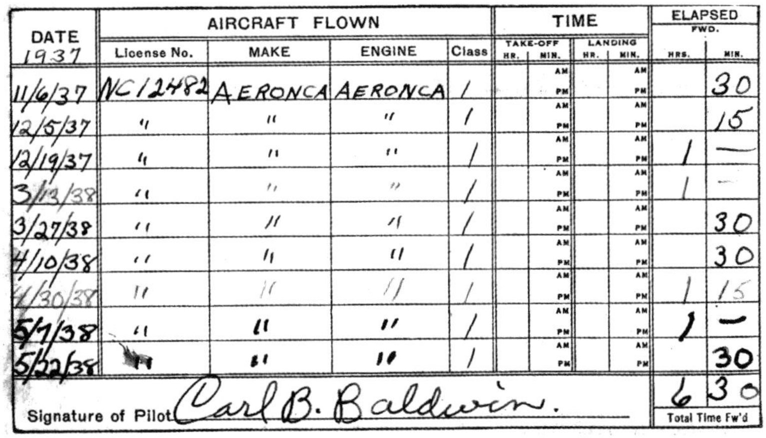

DATE 1937	AIRCRAFT FLOWN				TIME				ELAPSED FWD.	
	License No.	MAKE	ENGINE	Class	TAKE-OFF HR. MIN.		LANDING HR. MIN.		HRS.	MIN.
11/6/37	NC12482	AERONCA	AERONCA	1	AM PM		AM PM			30
12/5/37	"	"	"	1	AM PM		AM PM			15
12/19/37	"	"	"	1	AM PM		AM PM		1	—
3/13/38	"	"	"	1	AM PM		AM PM		1	—
3/27/38	"	"	"	1	AM PM		AM PM			30
4/10/38	"	"	"	1	AM PM		AM PM			30
4/30/38	"	"	"	1	AM PM		AM PM		1	15
5/1/38	"	"	"	1	AM PM		AM PM		1	—
5/22/38	"	"	"	1	AM PM		AM PM			30

Signature of Pilot *Carl B. Baldwin.* Total Time Fw'd 6 30

Form ACA 935

DEPARTMENT OF COMMERCE
CIVIL AERONAUTICS ADMINISTRATION
WASHINGTON

THIS IS TO IDENTIFY

Carl ___ Beecher ___ Baldwin
(First name) (Middle name) (Last name)

who has been certificated as an airman by the Civil Aeronautics Administration and whose signature appears hereon.

Signature *Carl Beecher Baldwin*

U. S. GOVERNMENT PRINTING OFFICE 16—25443-1

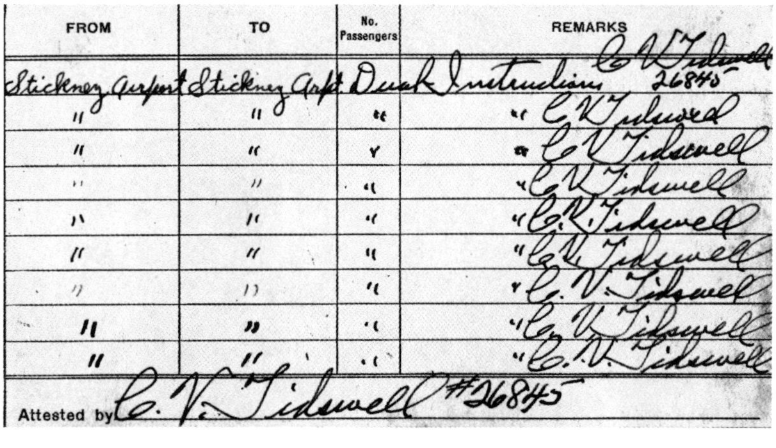

FROM	TO	No. Passengers	REMARKS
Stickney Airport	Stickney Arpt	Dual Instruction	C.V.Tidwell 26845
"	"	"	" C.V.Tidwell
"	"	Y	" C.V.Tidwell
"	"	"	" C.V.Tidwell
"	"	"	" C.V.Tidwell
"	"	"	" C.V.Tidwell
"	"	"	" C.V.Tidwell
"	"	"	" C.V.Tidwell
"	"	"	" C.V.Tidwell

Attested by *C. V. Tidwell* #26845

Carl Baldwin's Pilot Log showing time flying at Stickney Airport in 1937 and his identification from the Department of Commerce . Courtesy of Carl Baldwin.

Hoping for the lucrative United States Airmail contract to help make ends meet, Toledo's leaders were dismayed to learn that the airport was turned down. The Government cited high tension wires, the Ottawa River, and the rail yard as safety concerns. However, pilots flying the New York to Chicago leg of the transcontinental flight path were following beacon lights twenty-five miles apart and the lights of Toledo's business district would confuse the pilots when they made the fifteen mile detour to the north to land at the Stickney Airport. Toledo's first municipal airport was in operation only eight months when Transcontinental Airport [Metcalf Field] was opened. Located on the Cleveland to Chicago flight path the airport prospered.

After Toledo relinquished its lease in 1930 Toledo's own pioneer aviator Anthony [Toney] Nassr took over Stickney Field. One of Nassr's early flying partners was Roy Knabenshue who gained local fame in 1905 by landing an airship or dirigible on top of Toledo's Spitzer Building.

Toney Nassr's airship or dirigible in 1906. The postcard photo was taken by Toledoan L.A. Bush. Postcard courtesy of Ken Levin.

On one of Nassr's early balloon flights he got caught in the tall tree limb's of Bay View Park and was trapped there until some campers caught the draglines and safely pulled his craft to the ground.

Excellent photo of Nassr's airship showing the 45 foot spruce frame-work attached to the Japanese silk bags filled with helium. The postcard photo was taken by Toledoan L.A. Bush. Postcard courtesy of Ken Levin.

Looking south on Stickney Avenue past the Ottawa River. Stickney Municipal Airport was located on the left background of the photo. The photo was taken from the driveway of Peterson's Sohio Station. Courtesy of Charles and Katherine Stahl.

Robert Koleman was brought to Stickney Airport to handle the commercial aspects of the field in October of 1933 when Fremont native Earl Baskey leased the airport. Koleman wrote a monograph *Young Wings Over America* in which he reflected on his time at Stickney Airport.

FREE AIR SHOW
TOLEDO-STICKNEY AVE. AIRPORT
Sunday, July 22, 1934

PARACHUTE JUMP
STUNT FLYING

PASSENGER FLIGHTS $1.00
Over Downtown Toledo

Aerial Parade over City at Noon
FLYING INSTRUCTIONS
Fleet-Travel Air-Bird Airplanes Flight Instructors Transport Pilots

Admission and Parking Free

Come out and enjoy an afternoon of Aerial
Entertainment at
STICKNEY AVENUE AIRPORT

Coming to Toledo from Dayton in October of 1933, Toledo-Stickney Airport director Robert Koleman used this advertisement to bring business to his financially struggling airport. Courtesy of Robert Koleman's monograph *Young Wings Over America* published in 1979.

After Baskey relinquished the lease the field was known as Shell Field or as the Roger Q. William's Toledo Airport. Williams ran the Williams School of Aeronautics. Williams was well remembered by Winston Smith for his New York to Rome flight. The National Supply Company ran the air-strip until 1942.

With World War II in full swing the Government used the Stickney Avenue Airport land to build a plant for the Electric AutoLight Company to build and assemble critical airplane parts for the war effort.

The Jeep Corporation acquired title to the property in 1964 and used the former AutoLight plant along with the North Cove plant to build the increasingly popular Jeep. The hangar which at one time could house as many as 18 planes was in dire need of repairs. Used by the adjacent farmers to store their machinery, the hangar was refurbished and used as a temporary repair facility for completed Jeeps. The hangar was finally torn down in the late 90's.

The eighteen plane hangar that once graced the grass landing field of the Stickney Avenue Airport. Courtesy of the Toledo BLADE.

National Airport
Point Place's 3rd Airport

The northwest corner of Alexis and Telegraph which would eventually become the grass landing strip of the National Airport. Photo taken at a Fly-In on July 24, 1927. Courtesy of the Toledo Lucas County Public Library.

Aerial view of Alexis Road [left to right] **and Telegraph** [top left to bottom right]**, Detroit Avenue is the extreme upper right, and State Line Road runs across the top of the photo. National Airport is located in the upper center, and the discontinued Crabb Field is in the lower left. Circa 1930. Courtesy of the Toledo Lucas County Public Library.**

When the Stickney Avenue Airport or Shell Field closed for good in 1942, the Civilian Air Patrol shifted their base of operations to the National Airport at Alexis and Telegraph Roads. Home to many of the area's amateur pilots, the National Airport continued operations under the guidance of the Aiken Aircraft Corporation until 1960, when they were purchased by National Flight Services.

Harvey Mahrt, a veteran of 35 years in the aviation industry and owner, said that Amos Squire a flight instructor of long standing has many new ideas to improve the services that the airport has to offer.

One of the hangars at the National Airport. Courtesy of the Toledo Lucas County Public Library.

By 1961 National Flight Services had added a paved 3,000 foot runway and had developed a facility for converting aircraft for business use. The expanded hangar has room for 27 planes and more hangars are under construction to meet the demand. National Flight Services has three experienced pilots available for commercial flights and five veteran pilots serving as flight instructors. President of the growing airport Harvey Mahrt said *".. only one or two airports in the country can match our facilities here in Toledo."*

By July of 1965 many of the promised improvements were on public display as Marjorie Schaefer, Miss Toledo of 1964, cut the ribbon opening the public observation platform to the waiting spectators. Called the *Roost* the platform was located atop the refurbished main hangar fifty yards from the primary landing strip. From the *Roost* the other improvements became readily apparent. Parking for two hundred cars parallel to Alexis Avenue, and in front of the main hangars more than two acres were graded and paved for airplane parking. A fenced children's play area with a variety of outdoor gym equipment was added for their safety.

Looking south towards Toledo, this aerial view has Alexis Avenue running left to right with Telegraph Top to bottom. National Airport is in the lower left and an excellent view of the Telegraph Drive-In is in the lower right. Circa 1970. Courtesy of the Toledo Lucas County Public Library.

With their ten year lease due to expire in 1971, the National Flight Services recognized that the commercial development of the Alexis Road corridor was beginning to expand. Phillip Portteus, a noted Toledo developer, had proposed a shopping center for the National Airport property and the needed Zoning change was obtained from City Council in May of 1973. Several years later the Skyview National Plaza, later to be known as the NorthTowne Mall, began construction in March of 1978. After almost seventy years of aviation history the Alexis Telegraph corridor would never again hear the mellow exhaust of propeller driven planes.

Willow Beach or Cullen Park
Point Place's 4th Airport

Started in 1929 by Jimmy Hayes, the Fretti Brothers – Joe and Ben, and John McMahon Willow Beach remained a thriving picnic and recreational destination for thousands of Toledoans. With parking for three thousand cars, and for others just a street car ride away, Toledoans rushed to the sheltered groves of Willow Beach to welcome the cool breezes of Lake Erie. With mechanical rides for the kids, roller coaster and other thrill rides for the young adults, and organized gambling for the parents Willow Beach was a natural.

Willow Beach in July of 1949. The crowds are gone and the area has a tired and sleepy appearance. Courtesy of the Toledo BLADE.

That is until Point Place was annexed by the City of Toledo in 1937. With Toledo's anti-gambling stance the gamblers just walked away from their leased Willow Beach and retreated further into the confines of Washington Township. Reverting to its original owner, Frank Lux found himself trying to operate the amusement park in the midst of the Depression years. With falling revenue and dwindling crowds Frank decided to bring another attraction to Willow Beach to bring back the paying customers. He added a seaplane base after the end of World War II.

Lasting only a couple of years in operation not much is known about its early years. The base was located in the small cove adjacent to the current entrance into Cullen Park.

If you look closely there are two yellow J3 Piper Cubs with lightening strikes on their sides mounted on floats, an operations shack, and a Republic SeaBee on the right. Courtesy of the Point Place Heritage Society.

It wasn't till the early 70's that interest in a Seaplane Base resurfaced in Point Place. Float planes were active in the Point, and depending on whom you talk to there were any where from three to five planes that were based on the Ottawa River. Several planes were buoyed off Edgewater and 138th Street, and a couple of others were in the Lost Peninsula area.

Present day Cullen Park looking north from Summit Street. Keller's SeaPlane Base was located on the left center of the photograph. From the author's collection.

At the time of their application for a SeaPlane Base only Delaware and Dayton had operating bases in Ohio. The proposed site at the Cullen Park Marina has already been inspected by aviation officials, and their report indicated that it was a *"highly suitable and safe area for a park recreational facility."* The Ohio Division of Aviation was very anxious to have a SeaPlane Base in Toledo so that float planes would have access to the Lake Erie Islands.

With interest in a Sea-Plane Base running high and backing from the State of Ohio, Roger and Donna Keller opened their Sea-Plane Base in 1972 and received their certification in August of 1973.

Come ride with us. Courtesy of Roger Keller and Family.

Rates were $10.00 per person, Minimum three passengers per flight. Maximum five passengers. Children five and under half price. Rides 10 A.M. until dark Saturday, Sunday, and Holidays. With this coupon you could reduce the cost by one dollar. Courtesy of Roger Keller and Family.

The Keller SeaPlane Base at Cullen Park. Courtesy of Roger Keller and Family.

The SeaPlane Base was in operation for almost ten years ending in 1981.

Point Place & its many yesterdays
corrections

Inglasbe's Grocery Store was located at 124th Street and Summit in the northeast corner of the intersection. The store became the anchor for Edgewater Appliance and Furniture and is now the McDonalds restaurant property.

Lawson's Grocery Store on Edgewater Drive was not located at 145th Street and Edgewater Drive, but further investigation places Lawson's Store at 5929 Edgewater Drive which was the residence of Walt Duling in 1954. 5929 Edgewater Drive was the location of Walt's Boat Building facilities, or 141st Street and Edgewater Drive.

SNOWBOARDING

by Bob Woods

The Child's World

Published in the United States of America by The Child's World®
PO Box 326 • Chanhassen, MN 55317-0326 • 800-599-READ • www.childsworld.com

Content Adviser: Kurt Hoy, Editor, Transworld Snowboarding magazine, Oceanside, California

Acknowledgments

The Child's World®: Mary Berendes, Publishing Director

Editorial Directions, Inc.: E. Russell Primm, Editorial Director; Melissa McDaniel, Line Editor; Matt Messbarger, Project Editor and Editorial Assistant; Susan Hindman, Copy Editor; Susan Ashley, Proofreader; Terry Johnson, Olivia Nellums, Katharine Trickle, and Julie Zaveloff, Fact Checkers; Tim Griffin/IndexServ, Indexer; James Buckley Jr. and James Gigliotti, Photo Researchers and Selectors

Editorial and photo research services provided by Shoreline Publishing Group LLC, Santa Barbara, California

The Design Lab: Kathleen Petelinsek, Art Direction and Design; Kari Thornborough, Art Production

Photos

Cover: Digital Vision/Punchstock; Aaron Chang/Corbis: 28; Chris Trotman/Duomo/Corbis: 22; Corbis: 4, 11, 12; Duomo/Corbis: 8, 21, 24, 26; Getty Images: 17, 27; Jeff Curtes/Corbis: 7; Mike Chew/Corbis: 14; Reuters NewMedia Inc./Corbis: 25; Shawn Frederick/Corbis: 19.

Registration

Library of Congress Cataloging-in-Publication Data

Woods, Bob.
 Snowboarding / by Bob Woods.
   v. cm. — (Kids' guides)
 Includes bibliographical references (p.   ) and index.
 Contents: Get on board—Snowboarding's hard, cold history—Gearing up and go—Hit the slippery slopes—Snowboarding stars.
 ISBN 1-59296-211-4 (library bound : alk. paper) 1. Snowboarding—Juvenile literature. [1. Snowboarding.] I. Title. II. Series.
 GV857.S57W66 2005
 796.93'9—dc22   2003027365

9/26/05
25.00

CONTENTS

GET ON BOARD

Snowboarding has taken the extreme

sports world by storm. In fact, it's the fastest-growing sport in the world. There are more than six million boarders in the United States alone. Before long, they'll outnumber traditional skiers. What's amazing about this is that, until the 1990s, most ski resorts didn't even allow snowboarding.

Snowboarding is a radical combination of skateboarding and surfing, all done on snow-covered hills and mountains. Snowboarders—they like to call themselves riders or shredders—wear special boots that are strapped into a pair of **bindings** attached to a single board. The board consists of a wooden core sandwiched between several thin sheets of **fiberglass** and space age plastics covered with colorful graphics.

Snowboarding combines the fun of skiing and surfing at their most extreme.

Boarders glide down trails, weaving back and forth by shifting their weight from toe to heel and side to side.

From these basic moves, they perform dozens of outrageous
jumps, spins, flips, and other stunts such as the **grab.** Like
skateboarders, they sometimes do their thing in half-pipes.
The half-pipes used by snowboarders are U-shaped snow-and-ice
ditches carved into mountainsides. Certain resorts have built
snowboarder-only parks with special snowboarder-friendly
terrain. These parks include trails filled with ramps, rails,
jumps, and other obstacles for riders to use.

The huge growth of snowboarding has spawned competitions around the world. Proof of snowboarding's global popularity came at the 1998 Winter Games, where it became an official
Olympic sport.

Almost every Olympic snowboarder started out when he
or she was a kid. Today, many manufacturers make equipment
just for kids. In this book, we'll take you on a historic journey
way back to the 1960s and the "Snurfer" that started it all. We'll
show you the awesome boards, bindings, boots, and other gear
riders use. You'll learn the basics of how to ride, as well as some
gnarly stunts—and some shredder lingo. Finally, we'll intro-
duce you to some of the top snowboarders on the planet.

We can't promise that reading this book will make you a
world-class snowboarder. One thing we *can* guarantee, though,
is that you won't be . . . um . . . bored!

CHAPTER one

SNOWBOARDING'S COLD, HARD HISTORY

People have been sliding along on the
snow since, well, the Ice Age. But no one thought of snowboarding until Christmas Day 1965 in a backyard in Michigan. A man
named Sherman Poppen was watching his little girl, Wendy, try
to stand up on her sled, when he had a wild idea. He ran down to
the corner drugstore and bought a pair of kids' skis. He fastened
them together. He put a rope at the nose so his daughter could
hold it and stay stable. Wendy stood on it, and off she slid, into
winter sports history.

Taking his wife's suggestion, Poppen combined the words
snow and *surf* and dubbed his new contraption the Snurfer.
Before long, all the kids in the neighborhood wanted one. Poppen
couldn't make them fast enough, so he sold his idea to Bruns-
wick, a huge sporting goods company. By the mid-1970s, nearly
half a million Snurfers had been sold, and Snurfing became a
cult craze among kids and teens. Some ski resorts even held
Snurfing contests.

Those bitten by the Snurfer bug included several guys
who improved on Poppen's invention. Influenced by surfboard
designs, they developed what would become known as snowboards. In 1975, Dimitrije Milovich came up with one he called
the Winterstick. Tom Sims was a skateboarding kid in eighth

grade when he built his own snowboard so he would have something to ride in the winter. He founded Sims Snowboards in
1977. Chris Sanders founded Avalanche Snowboards in 1982.
Mike Olson quit college in 1984 to start Gnu. And then there's
Jake Burton Carpenter, whose Burton Snowboards has become
the biggest name in the business.

     In the 1980s, snowboarding gained popularity around
the world. By the end of the decade, championship competitions were held in the United States and Europe. The media
ran stories about this "extreme sport," and magazines such

Ski resorts
have had to
make room for
the soaring
popularity of
snowboarding.

Snowboarding competitions are a rapidly growing fan favorite.

as *Transworld Snowboarding* appeared on newsstands. Professional and amateur organizations were formed. They created races, established rules, and represented the growing numbers of snowboarders. In 1992, the United States Ski Association added snowboarding to its responsibilities.

Meanwhile, manufacturers kept improving snowboards.

Early models were sculpted from wood; some had fins on the bottom like a water ski. The introduction of high-tech plastics and metal edges made boards faster and easier to **maneuver.** Improvements in bindings and boots increased comfort and safety.

As the boards got better, so did the boarders riding them. Teenagers looking for thrills beyond those found on two skis were drawn to the sport. Skateboarders and surfers found it easy to cross over to this wintry pastime. Young, athletic, and daring, they had no fear of performing flips, grabs, 180s, and other amazing tricks. Boarding in baggy pants and parkas, with loud rock music blaring from outdoor speakers, they created a fun-loving, grungy subculture.

The problem, however, was that, at first, most ski areas wouldn't allow snowboarders on their slopes. The boarders were just too radical for the traditionalists. But as boarding continued to grow faster than skiing, the resorts couldn't resist the new business. One by one, the resorts welcomed boarders, luring them with snowboard parks featuring half-pipes and **slalom** courses.

Today, the number of snowboarders in the United States—mostly kids and teens—goes up every year. Burton, Gnu, and other major ski makers now also sell millions of dollars worth of

CHAIRMAN OF THE BOARDERS

Jake Burton Carpenter grew up on Long Island, near New York City. From an early age, he loved to snow ski. In the mid-1960s, he bought a Snurfer and was instantly hooked on riding a single board down snowy hills. But there was more to it for him. "From the time I was 14 until I graduated from college, I always thought I could turn my Snurfing hobby into a business," he told *Fortune* magazine.

Carpenter tinkered with various snowboard designs before launching Burton Snowboards in Burlington, Vermont, in 1977. The business struggled for several years because most people didn't know about the sport and most ski resorts wouldn't let boarders on their slopes. Carpenter hung in there, though, and sales started skyrocketing in the mid-1980s. In 2003, nearly one in three snowboards sold was a Burton. The name is also big in Europe and Asia. Burton, which is constantly improving the designs and ways of producing snowboards, also has a line of bindings, boots, clothing, and accessories.

Carpenter does a lot to promote the sport of snowboarding, including teaching people how to ride. "I teach about 10 to 20 people a year who have never ridden before," he says, "and I think I enjoy it as much as they do." The company sponsors a team of professional riders, and two of its stars, Ross Powers and Kelly Clark, won gold medals at the 2002 Winter Olympics in Salt Lake City, Utah.

snowboarding gear. They make gear for kids and adults, beginners and pros, racers and freestylers. From the Ice Age to the space age, snowboarding has evolved into one of the hottest extreme sports of all time.

CHAPTER two

GEAR UP AND GO

Just as the extreme sport of snow-

boarding has grown by leaps and bounds, the equipment options
have expanded, too. So before you buy a board, it's smart to do
your homework. Learn about the different types of gear and
what fits your body and skill level. Once you're properly outfit-
ted, scope out snowboarding areas and the types of trails where
you can enjoy yourself the most.

Explore your
options and find
the board that's
right for you.

When it comes to the ABCs of equipment, stop at the

letter B: boards, bindings, and

boots. The selection might seem

endless, but you'll be able to

narrow it down once you have

an idea of what fits your needs.

(Hint: it's a good idea to first rent

a few different packages to deter-

mine which combination is right

for you.)

Boards

Specialty shops and sporting goods

stores sometimes have snowboards

from more than 30 different

A good sporting-goods store can help you with boards and other equipment.

companies. Just because a board looks cool doesn't mean it's right for you. The one you purchase should be for someone your age, height, weight, and level of experience, as well as matched to the type of terrain you prefer. Price is a factor, too, considering that a board can cost from about $200 up to $700!

Beginners often start with a **freeride** board, good for riding all types of mountain trails. Look for a softer, more flexible board rather than a stiff one. Standing on end, it should come up at least to your chin. When you're standing on it, it should be wide enough that your toes or heels don't hang over the side.

Freestyle boards are the same size at both ends and can be ridden both forward and **fakie.** They're good for both beginners and more experienced boarders who do tricks and jumps. Stiff alpine boards are designed for racing.

Bindings

The most common bindings consist of a hard base plate, a high back piece, and straps that go across the front to secure your boots. You can also buy step-in bindings, without straps, which are easier to put on but can limit your control. Alpine racers who want extra edge control use simpler-looking plate bindings, which include a base plate, steel bails (half hoops), and a heel or toe lever. Be sure your boots match your type of bindings.

Boots

Boots greatly affect your control—and therefore enjoyment—on the snowboard, so choose wisely. Boots come in three basic types. The most popular are soft boots. They feature a padded inner boot, sometimes called a bladder, which keeps your feet

dry and warm. The outer boot is more rigid. Both have laces. Tightened separately, they ensure a snug fit. Soft boots are easy to walk around in when you're not on a board.

Hard boots look like traditional ski boots. They too have a padded inner boot, but they have a hard plastic shell on the outside, which tightens with buckles, and a hard sole.

Step-in boots, which have a soft upper boot and hard sole, are made specifically for step-in bindings.

A snowboarder's clothing often is as colorful as his (or her) stunts.

Clothing

Snowboarders love to show off both their skills and their look. Underneath their colorful outer gear is the stuff that anyone venturing out in freezing weather should have: thermal under-

BOARDERS WELCOME

Snowboarding is America's fastest-growing sport. Just about anywhere there's snow, there are boarders. Most every ski resort in North America grooms trails just for snowboarders, and many set up special parks with half-pipes, ramps, and race courses. Both *Transworld Snowboarding* and *Snowboarder* magazines (and their Web sites) provide helpful guides to resorts, mountains, and parks.

Make sure to check the signs and rules before you take off. And some trails are too dangerous during certain winter conditions. Always check with the experts before going onto a new trail.

wear and socks to keep them warm and dry. The second layer includes a fleece jacket or sweater, and loose-fitting, waterproof snowboarding pants. The final touch is a waterproof, windproof jacket, plus insulated gloves (to help break inevitable spills). Snowboarding pants and jackets come in a wild variety of colors and designs. You'll look like a bright rainbow against the white snow.

Safety Gear

Protect your head and ears from the elements with a hat. Whether you're into funky or fundamental, you have dozens of styles to choose from. Goggles cut the sun's glare, the wind's chill, and the snow's cold. If you're racing, or to be totally safe, wear a snowboarding helmet.

CHAPTER three

HIT THE SLIPPERY SLOPES

Now that you're familiar with the

history of snowboarding, the gear you'll need to join in, and places to board, it's time to actually get out there and do it. If you're already a snow skier, skateboarder, or surfer, it might be a bit easier to cross over to snowboarding. Regardless of your experience on or off the slopes, every newcomer can benefit from taking lessons. Most winter sports resorts have a snowboarding school. There are also camps, clinics, and coaches all over snow country.

For beginners, the main goal is to get down the trail in one piece. Falling is part of the deal, so don't be afraid to eat some snow. And if you're dressed properly, getting wet or cold shouldn't be a worry either.

Before starting out, you'll first need to determine whether, like most people, your stance on the board is "regular"—with your left foot forward—or "goofy"—with your right foot forward. One or the other should feel natural when you try it. If in doubt, ask your instructor for help.

Start out on a flat surface area. While sitting down, strap your front foot onto the board. Keep the heel edge dug slightly into the snow. Stand up, and using your free back foot, kick the board forward, as you would a skateboard. This skating action comes in handy when crossing flat areas.

Then, with both feet in the bindings, it's time to get moving down a hill. Maintaining your balance can be frustrating at first. But by shifting your weight forward and backward and from side to side, you'll be gliding and turning within a day or

It takes some practice to get used to turning and balancing.

two. Once you get used to the action, try a heel-side stop. Turn the board uphill by gradually putting your weight on your heels. After you've slowed down enough, dig the rear of the snowboard into the snow. Next, try riding fakie. Head down the hill leading with the foot that's usually in the rear.

These are some basics of freeriding, the style preferred by most beginners. Sometimes called all-mountain riding, freeriding allows you to master riding on most any kind of terrain. You can freeride in hard-packed or powder snow conditions, while doing some jumps and sharp turns, or **carves.** Experienced boarders can graduate to more difficult freestyle boarding. This may include spectacular jumps, spins, flips, and other maneuvers performed on ramps, rails, and half-pipes—stuff you might see watching the X Games, the Gravity Games, or the Olympics on TV. Alpine boarding, for expert riders, is all about speed and deep carving down steep slalom courses.

No matter to what extreme you take snowboarding, you should know about some gnarly tricks—and cool lingo— that make the sport so awesome. On the surface of the slope, riding fakie can lead to 180- and 360-degree turns. An **ollie** is performed by lifting the front foot first and then the back foot to spring up and catch some air. Lift the back foot first

Don't try this at home! Experienced snowboarders can make some thrilling moves.

for the similarly named nollie. When airborne, turn 180 degrees for an air-to-fakie. Airborne grabs, where you literally grab the board with one or both hands, are big crowd pleasers.

Let's rip over to the half-pipe, where there's a lot of high-flying action. It's called a half-pipe because it resembles a round pipe cut in half, although the bottom is flat. Riders enter from the top, drop down one side, and then glide up the opposite curved wall, called a transition, or "trannie." They catch air by gathering enough speed to zoom up beyond the lip of the wall and then turn back down. Experienced free-stylers go even higher and do aerial stunts such as an Indy grab, an alley-oop, a 360 spin, a McTwist, and a crippler.

You won't be doing those tricks when you start, but even the world's best boarders began on the bunny hill!

ETIQUETTE AND SAFETY

Unless you venture off the beaten path into the **backcountry** with a couple of buddies, you'll be snowboarding at a resort with lots of other boarders and skiers. Be courteous toward others and avoid collisions. If you need to slow down or stop on a run, get to the side—and watch behind you. Learn how to read the trail map and signs indicating easy, intermediate, and difficult runs. Stay on the marked trails. Never ride hard into an unknown area.

CHAPTER four

SNOWBOARDING STARS

Unlike baseball or football, snowboarding

is a new sport, so it doesn't have a long history of stars. The

pioneers of the 1960s and 1970s were mostly just riding for fun.

But as more and more people started snowboarding, competi-

tions began to flourish.

In the 1990s, the sport skyrocketed in popularity.

Big-time competitions heated up throughout the United

States, Canada, and Europe, and snowboard superstars

emerged. When the sport was
added to the Winter Olympic
Games in 1998, snowboard-
ing was finally ready for prime-
time television. Top boarders
can also take part
in the Winter X Games,
World Cup races, the U.S.
Snowboard Grand Prix, and
other major events.

The ultimate goal for
many snowboarders is an
Olympic gold medal. But the
Winter Games are held only

Snowboarding's
booming popularity
is evident at the
Winter X Games.

The last two Winter Olympic Games have included snowboarding.

every four years. That leaves snowboarders plenty of time in between to strut their stuff elsewhere. The USA Snowboard Association (USASA) holds competitions at resorts across the country for adults, teens, and kids of all ages, from **novices** to experts. Top riders from different regions qualify to compete at USASA's national championships.

The U.S. Ski and Snowboard Association (USSA) works with the U.S. Olympic Committee to develop athletes for national and international competition. These athletes take part in World Cup events and the Olympic Games. USSA organizes several series of snowboarding events across the country for qualified riders. From those ranks, USSA selects members of its men's and women's U.S. National Snowboard Team.

Both racing and freestyle events are held at most competitions. The racing events are slalom, giant slalom, super G (super giant slalom), and snowboardcross (often called boardercross or SBX). In slalom, boarders race on a downhill course through gates. Giant slalom uses a longer course with gates set farther apart. The course is stretched even more in super G, where racers reach speeds of up to 45 miles (72 kilometers) per hour. In SBX, four to six riders zoom through an obstacle course that includes banked turns, gates, jumps, and more. The first two or three finishers advance to the next round of competition and eventually the championship race.

Freestyle events include big air, the half-pipe, and slopestyle. In big air competition, riders catch as much air as possible from a ramp or hill and perform tricks. In the half-pipe, boarders do tricks while weaving up and down the vertical walls and in the air. The slopestyle event features riders trying to stick tricks while navigating a downhill obstacle course that includes rails, jumps, and even mailboxes!

American boarders won five gold medals at the Salt Lake City Olympics in 2002. Ross Powers and Kelly Clark took the half-pipe golds. In fact, Americans swept the men's half-pipe,

The Olympics showcase the amazing athletic skills of snow-boarders.

American Ross Powers is one of the world's best snowboarders.

with Danny Kass and Jarret Thomas winning the silver and bronze.

Powers was already a legend long before he arrived in Salt Lake City. The Vermont native started boarding when he was seven. At age 19, he won the bronze medal in the half-pipe at the Olympics in 1998, the same year he took first place in the half-pipe and slopestyle at the X Games.

Clark, a fellow Vermonter, was just a year out of high school at the 2002 Olympics when she wowed the half-pipe

Kelly Clark was a gold-medal winner at the 2002 Olympics.

judges. The last rider in the event, she nailed a pair of jumps,

a 540-degree inverted spin called a McTwist, and a 720-degree

spin to easily blow away the competition.

More young-sters than ever before are getting into snowboarding.

American snowboarders to keep an eye on at the next Winter Olympics are Seth Wescott, an SBX specialist; 17-year-old Shaun White, winner of the 2003 U.S. Open slopestyle event; and Andy Finch, the top half-pipe rider at the 2003 World Cup Championships. On the women's side, watch out for Gretchen Bleiler, a daredevil on the half-pipe, and 2003 U.S. Open overall winner Hannah Teter.

In just a couple of decades, snowboarding time-tripped from nowhere to everywhere at warp speed. And there's no sign of it slowing down. Predictions are that boarders will soon outnumber skiers in the United States. And as the equipment improves with the skills of riders, expect jumps to get bigger, taking boarders ever higher to perform even greater tricks. One thing that won't change, however, is the extreme fun that this sport brings to everyone involved.

Snowboarding is fun and it's cool—and you can't beat the views!

THE STATES OF SNOWBOARDING

Mountains and snow are the main ingredients for a snowboarding resort. So it's not surprising that most resorts are located in mountainous states. These include Colorado, Vermont, California, Oregon, and Montana. In Canada, the western province of British Columbia is a hot snowboarding destination. Just about every winter resort welcomes snowboarders, with special trails, terrain parks, half-pipes, and equipment rentals. Of course, some are better than others. *Transworld Snowboarding* magazine polled its readers to learn their 10 favorite resorts. Here are the results:

1. Whistler/Blackcomb, British Columbia
   www.whistler.com
2. Mammoth Mountain, Mammoth Lakes, California
   www.mammothmountain.com
3. Breckenridge, Colorado
   www.breckenridge.snow.com
4. Vail, Colorado
   www.vail.com
5. Timberline, Timberline Lodge, Oregon
   www.timberlinelodge.com
6. Snow Summit, Big Bear Lake, California
   www.snowsummit.com
7. Mount Hood Meadows, Mount Hood, Oregon
   www.skihood.com
8. Copper Mountain, Colorado
   www.coppercolorado.com
9. Mount Snow, Vermont
   www.mountsnow.com
10. Okemo Mountain, Ludlow, Vermont
    www.okemo.com

GLOSSARY

backcountry—A skiing or snowboarding area that is not marked by regular trails within ski resort boundaries.

bindings—Devices that attach your boots to the snowboard.

carves—Wide, sweeping turns that take a rider back and forth across a slope.

fakie—Riding the snowboard backward down a hill.

fiberglass—A strong material made from fine threads of glass, used in buildings, cars, boats, snowboards, and other things.

freeride—A type of snowboarding that does not involve obstacles.

gnarly—Difficult, crazy, or just plain stupid.

grab—A snowboard trick in which the rider reaches down to hold the board with one hand.

maneuver—To move something carefully into a particular position.

novices—People who are new to an activity.

ollie—A skateboarding trick that has been adapted for snowboarding. You pop the board up into the air while both feet are on it.

slalom—A race that involves riding back and forth around gates set up on a slope.

FIND OUT MORE

On the Web

Visit our home page for lots of links about snowboarding:
http://www.childsworld.com/links.html

NOTE TO PARENTS, TEACHERS, AND LIBRARIANS: We routinely check
our Web links to make sure they're safe, active sites—so encourage your
readers to check them out!

Books

Bennett, Jeff, Charles Arnell, and Scott Downey. *The Complete Snowboarder.*
Camden, Me.: Ragged Mountain Press, 1994.

Christopher, Matt. *Snowboard Showdown.* Boston: Little, Brown & Company,
1999.

Crossingham, John. *Snowboarding in Action.* New York: Crabtree Publishing
Company, 2002.

Fraser, Andy. *Snowboarding.* Chicago: Heinemann Library, 2000.

Herran, Joe, and Ron Thomas. *Snowboarding.* Philadelphia: Chelsea House,
2003.

Stone, Tanya Lee. *Snowboards: From Start to Finish.* Woodbridge, Conn.:
Blackbirch Press, 2000.

INDEX

About the Author

Bob Woods is a freelance writer in Madison, Connecticut. Over the past 20 years, his work has appeared in many magazines, including *Sports Illustrated*. He has written books for young readers about Barry Bonds, Shaquille O'Neal, the National Football League, NASCAR history, and other sports topics.